W9-BKJ-656

The God Within

Sara,
the "Love"
Love the "Love"
within.

Tom Allender

The
God Within

Our Journey Towards
A Personal God

By
Father Tom Allender, S.J.

MW Publishing, L.L.C., Phoenix, Arizona, U.S.A.

FIRST EDITION

The ideas and suggestions expressed in this book are intended to be an aid on your spiritual journey. People suffering from addictions or the clinically depressed may need to first seek professional help before implementing the suggestions in this book.

MW Publishing, L.L.C., Phoenix 85030
Copyright ©1996 by MW Publishing, L.L.C.

All rights reserved under International and Pan-American Copyright Conventions. No part of this book may be reproduced or utilized in any form or by any means, electronic or mechanical, including photocopying, recording, or by any information storage or retrieval system, without permission in writing from the Publisher.

Printed in the United States of America.
First Edition

ISBN 0-9653261-0-1

Library of Congress Catalog Card Number: CIP 96-77102

        Allender, Tom
        The God Within: Our Journey Towards a Personal God
          by Father Tom Allender
        No index.

Inquires should be addressed to:

MW Publishing, L.L.C.
P.O. Box 3678
Phoenix, Arizona 85030
602.241.1407 FAX/Voice

Cover design by Neal Berg, Neal Berg Design.
Book layout by Matthew Ferguson, MT Consultants.

To My Family

*Our deepest fear is not
that we are inadequate.
Our deepest fear is that we
are powerful beyond measure.
It is our light, not our darkness, that most
frightens us. We ask ourselves, Who am I to be
brilliant, gorgeous, talented and fabulous?*

*Actually, who are you not to be?
You are a child of God.
Your playing small doesn't serve the world.
There's nothing enlightened about shrinking so that
other people won't feel insecure around you.
We were born to make manifest
the glory of God that is within us.
It's not just in some of us: it's in everyone.
And as we let our light shine,
we unconsciously give other people
permission to do the same.
As we are liberated from our own
fear, our presence automatically
liberates others.*

**Nelson Mandela
1994 Inaugural Speech**

CONTENTS

ACKNOWLEDGMENTS

I considered for many years turning my thoughts and sermons into a book but always realized it would be nearly impossible to do the job single-handedly. When I finally turned to the task, I was fortunate to have an able team to help. I thank Tom Eldridge for his help with the initial phase of this book. Thanks to Ron and Jo Ann Watkins for their assistance in organizing the manuscript.

I also want to thank Don Fisher for challenging me to enter into Life's Journey ministry and for the many hours of support as we worked through the audio and video material we have created together. Thanks to Dan and Jeannie Fisher for keeping me well supplied with tapes and running our office for the last twelve years. Thanks to the many wonderful people I have encountered on my journey — they have been some of my greatest teachers.

Finally, my deepest gratitude to the Society of Jesus for their constant love and faith in me.

INTRODUCTION

My personal crises with God came after I had been a Jesuit for twenty-six years and had been a recovering alcoholic for eight years. I had just left an assignment at a large parish where my days were filled with endless activities. I would baptize in the morning and console the victims of a suicide in the afternoon. For every wedding I performed, I counseled a couple who wanted to end their marriage. "I administered the sacraments of the Church to many people who had no appreciation of their significance." I collapsed into bed at night exhausted from work and yet my sleep was restless.

When a priest comes to know a family through a wedding, baptism or death, he becomes a part of that family and all families have religious needs. With every wedding I performed I added a new family to my growing list. While working, I received countless daily telephone calls and performed as many as one hundred weddings a year. I sometimes felt like a mindless functionary, pouring the gas of grace into too many empty spiritual tanks.

By 1984 I was exhausted and took a year sabbatical. I spent the time largely walking the beaches of Santa Barbara, California. Up to then, I had been so busy I hadn't realized that something was fundamentally wrong with me. I had always been a rescuer, both a man and a priest who felt overly responsible for the lives of others. Now for the first time in my life, I was free of responsibility with no one to rescue, no cause in which to become immersed. I was alone with my own thoughts and concerns and was compelled for the first time to face myself.

I had taken this sabbatical anticipating a positive experience but soon found that was not the case. I walked in the sand, listened to the surf, felt the ocean breeze on my face but found no solace. The effect of this solitude and of my sobriety was to heighten my perception of the spiritual wasteland in which I found myself. I knew that I needed to ground my faith and slowly turned inward to confront my own relationship with God.

I was forced to acknowledge that for too long I had been preaching a form of humanism, and in my newly found candor I faced the realization that though I was a priest I had no faith in a personal God.

I often preached a God of love, that we must love ourselves without conditions, and from that experience we give our love away to others. I told others to forgive and be gentle with themselves. People often told me that I had changed their lives, but I had never applied the lessons of spirituality from my sermons to myself. No one judged himself more harshly than I judged myself.

Throughout my life I realized I had not been personally honest. I had never made the inner connection with God that I intuitively craved. In my personal life I was shut off from others and I trusted no one. Every Christmas I received hundreds of cards but could count only a handful of people as real friends.

I discovered the gift of honesty with self on that beach, and I slowly began to face my distant relationship with God. I realized that to really understand, I must start at my beginning, with my own childhood, with my alcoholic family, and with the relationship I had with my parents. It is from that difficult self-examination that I at last began a personal relationship with God and from that experience comes this book.

When I resumed my ministry, I soon gave my first mission based on what I had discovered about God, relationships, and spirituality. In the years since, I have crisscrossed the nation traveling to more than four hundred parishes, and have given hundreds of missions to over two million people. I am constantly examining my models and over the years have expanded and modified them as I have received greater understanding. In many ways I still struggle in the wilderness seeking the light, but with each passing year the light becomes brighter.

This book, a response to countless requests, is the message I bring: How to find your personal God. It is the good news that I have discovered about spirituality in our modern lives. This revelation has given my life greater meaning, and I know that it can do the same for you.

Chapter One

THE ETERNAL JOURNEY

1

Several years ago a friend of mine became a deacon. Though he was ordained in August he was not asked to preach at mass until Holy Family Sunday, the first Sunday following Christmas. It seemed appropriate to the pastor that a family man should deliver that Sunday's homily. My friend decided to examine the words of Jesus and learn from the Gospels what he had to say about the family. A few days later I received a distressed call. "Tom," he said, stunned from his discovery, "I've read the words of Jesus in the scripture, and he has almost nothing to say about the family." Indeed, some of his comments he had found could be taken as contrary to the family.

For example, when Jesus was informed that his mother was waiting for him outside, he told the disciples that his mother is "whoever does the will of my Father." Another time Jesus said that unless you are willing to leave your father and mother, you could not be one of his disciples.

✝

After this conversation I gave the matter considerable thought because my friend had placed his finger on something I had realized for years without understanding the significance. There was, in fact, a great deal about which Jesus had nothing to say. He doesn't speak of war or of sexuality. When it comes to government, he tells us to render unto Caesar as though the matter is of no great importance.

Then it struck me. It was as if I cried aloud, "Eureka!" Jesus said so little about the affairs of this world because he was focused on eternal life. His message concerns our personal relationship with God and with his love. His message had always been before me in all its simplicity; only now I could understand it. For Jesus, every event in our lives, especially the pain and suffering, is to bring us to the point in life's journey where we realize that what makes us precious is not how we look, not what we do, nor what we own. What makes us precious is the love inside each one of us. We have not been created to be successful, to achieve status, or to acquire money. The reason we were created is to discover that love within and to share it with the people that God sends into our lives. Once we have entered into that love, we enter eternal life because God is love; God cannot die and love cannot die.

This was the revelation that most simplified my life. We are on a journey in which we reach no destination. It is a journey of discovery and along its path are way stations of insight. This is what the spiritual journey is about.

For example, when I worked at a Jesuit high school, I soon realized that many of these young men had no great interest in spiritual matters. What they sought was a good education so that they could have a lucrative career and acquire the material things of this world. This was, I realized, as I should have expected, for if they had it together at such a young age, what they would do with the rest of their lives? I uttered a silent prayer for these students. I hoped when the day came and they were ready to learn about God, someone would be there to teach them.

In life we find the best example of this unconditional love in the relationship of grandparents with their grandchildren. They, not parents, are the true teachers of spirituality in a family because, hopefully, they have grown spiritually from a lifetime of experience. I remember my dad playing with his grandchildren and talking baby talk. By the time his grandchildren came along, he had become more spiritual. He realized that what was most important was who he was to his grandchildren, not what material things he could give them.

In my life, I owe my faith more to my Irish grandmother than I do to anyone else. She was the first person who treated me like I was precious. I listened to every word she said as if it was the gospel. I could do no wrong in her eyes. She treated me as though I could walk on water. She loved me without conditions — just the way I was. Often the people who first treat you as precious become the most important people in your life, for it is they who first gave you unconditional love. It is from that experience, most often found in our grandparents, where the seeds of God's love are first planted.

I am reminded of this when I am asked to visit the dying. I will arrive prepared to comfort and console. Yet, often these dying persons have been my greatest teachers of faith. Recently, I entered a bedroom, and the man looked at me with peaceful eyes. "Father," he said, "I'm ready." At that moment I realized the man's whole life had been a preparation for this final surrender. Most people die the way they have lived; therefore, one of the most important events of our life is how we die.

Wouldn't it be wonderful if on our deathbed, we had accepted that God is love and that love is forever. Think of the inner peace to have discovered life's meaning.

Today we live in a society that preaches just the opposite. Our cultural values say we are special because of what we do, what degrees we have acquired, and what house we own. It is not who we are, but what we have that determines our worth. This is the great lie to which we are exposed daily. All we have to do is look at what we've done to Jesus at Christmas. We've made Jesus responsible for the economy.

I believe my generation enjoyed Christmas a lot more than kids do today. We had a lot fewer things, but a lot more family.

But the world as we know it is falling apart. Not that many years ago we witnessed the collapse of *Communism* and breathed a universal sigh of relief. Yet our own culture is so focused on greed, on what I call me-ism, that a collapse of our own society is all but inevitable.

Recently my car broke down in a strange city, and I was apprehensive about having it fixed. I was afraid they'd repair things that didn't need fixing. I paid five hundred dollars for the repair, and as I drove away the car broke down in exactly the same manner as it had two days before. I really wasn't surprised. Not too many years ago a major league baseball player said that he didn't know if he could play ball for three million dollars a year. I remember when I was in high school, I would have paid to be in the majors.

Where this selfishness has most affected us is in our families. If there is any lesson to be taken from history, it is that when the family fails, society collapses. That is what is taking place right now. Family is the most basic unit of society. When it falls apart, society falls apart.

Yet when future historians write of this period of history, I don't think they'll write of the collapse of our society. They will record instead that this was an epoch of great spiritual growth, for it is in troubled times that people search for meaning in their lives. Unlike the 1950s we no longer believe we have all the answers. Times of moral ambiguity, of family collapse, times of hedonism and materialism are also times when we most need God.

Wherever I go, I find this great thirst for spirituality. It is precisely because we have so much that we know something is missing.

There are two basic reasons why spirituality is important in our lives. First, life is especially difficult today. Whenever I see our teenagers, I have no wish to be fifteen years old again, even if I could have all the wisdom I've accrued during my life. While growing up I attended a Catholic grade school with more than eight hundred students. I can remember only one kid who came from a divorced home. The last time I taught in a Catholic school, fifty-five percent of the students came from divorced homes. It's not easy to be a young person today.

It's also very difficult to be a young married couple. Once the children arrive, the couple becomes preoccupied with the external world. Mom becomes a taxi driver, and everyone is going in different directions.

Life is difficult. A few years ago my dad passed away. Nothing in life prepares us for the death of a parent. It was painful for me, but what made it even more painful was seeing the effects of my dad's death on my mom. I would have done anything in the world to have eased her pain. They were married for fifty-four years, and her nights were never longer than those following the death of her husband. She went on a diet and walked for exercise every day. She did all she could to create positive energy, but the pain and suffering was still there for a long time.

This experience with my mom served to reinforce a lesson of life that I have come to understand. It is from pain that comes spiritual growth. It is from our suffering that we discover who we are. It is in life's struggles where we discover how precious life is. It is in life's travails where we find a personal God.

But, many people think they are going to eternal life in a limousine. When people bring me their problems, they often complain about life being unfair. They think life should be one rosy day after another. It is not and never will be.

The second reason why spirituality is important in our lives today is because none of us is perfect. We are all sinners. Each of us has a shadow, a dark side with warts and secrets. If anyone were to look hard enough at any one of us, they could find something wrong — or something precious. The spiritual point here isn't to emphasize that we are sinners, but rather to ask: Have we let God love us as we really are? Have we found God's love on the inside?

This is the theme of my book. It is precisely in nurturing the person inside us that we find God's love and discover the meaning of Jesus. I don't just talk about this in theory but show you how to do it. The journey to make our God personal is the same journey we take in becoming our own best friend.

What makes this journey so important is that all of our relationships are mirrors of our own relationship with ourselves and our God. We will never discover true intimacy in our married life or our family life until we have first found it within ourselves. We can't give it on the outside if we don't have it on the inside. I've performed marriage counseling for more than thirty years and have discovered that if one of the partners doesn't want to deal with the real problems in the marriage, the partner will project those issues onto the spouse. They don't want to take a good look at themselves. If parents don't deal with the real issues of their marriage, they project those issues onto their children. It is in this way that problems are passed on from generation to generation.

This is a book about connections, to help you see things in a new way, from a new vantage point. This message becomes more relevant and meaningful with each passing day. In our society it is imperative that we become strong on the inside, or we will be overwhelmed by the anger and meanness of our times, by the selfishness and greed to which we are subjected on the outside. Yet it is this very outside pressure that leads us to inner growth, growth that is unlikely to happen without it.

SPIRITUALITY

I define spirituality as developing reactions to our reactions. Let me explain what I mean. Whenever anyone injures me, hurts my feelings or my pride, my immediate reaction is to respond with the "silent treatment." You hurt me so I pretend you don't exist. The end result is that you feel guilty.

Everything we do on the outside is a reflection of what's on the inside. All of us have programmed reactions because of the way we were brought up. They're part of our family system. We need a process to go from our conditioned reactions to a new response to these reactions. This process is to surrender to God's love within us and in so doing bring God into our response to others. Once implemented these new reactions will remake our world.

For example, when I decide in my heart to accept a God of love within rather than experience the god of punishment, I tell myself I will no longer suffer from guilt. I will no longer beat myself up over my shortcomings. From now on God's love will help me grow from unpleasant experiences. I learn how to become a better person from my brokenness. When someone I love injures me (and all the people I love do so regularly because, like me, they're not perfect), instead of using the silent treatment or seeking to punish, I will offer an open heart rather than a wall that blocks love. Now we can both grow.

All of us have injured people we love. What a difference it makes when someone is there to meet us on the human journey, to help us grow rather than to make us feel more guilty for our failings. The difference in our reaction is whether we have within us a God of love or a god of punishment.

Making the decision to experience love, not anger, is only the first step. Living and practicing love requires effort; it requires that we change our thinking. We can utter a million decades of the rosary, go to mass every morning, and know the scriptures by heart, but if we don't do the work on the inside, nothing is going to change outwardly.

Spirituality is about how we do that work, how we accept the love on the inside and begin to let it direct the way we live. Spirituality is bringing the God of love into our reactions.

We must learn to replace anger with love and punishment with forgiveness. Forgiveness offers us a clean slate and a chance to begin anew. We can forgive ourselves because God forgives us. We can love ourselves and believe in our preciousness because God's love is within us. It is a river whose flow is eternal. If we are to tap into that flow, we must first locate its well-spring within ourselves.

The decision to change the way we relate to ourselves will lead us to the inner journey, the spirituality lying dormant within us all.

Chapter Two
THE TOOLS OF SPIRITUALITY

2

Many people consider themselves to be religious Christians. They attend church each week; they are familiar with the scriptures and read them routinely. And these are good practices. The greater issue, however, is: Are they spiritual Christians? Put another way: Are they Christians on the inside?

Spirituality isn't a spectator sport. We can't merely read books about the subject and discuss conceptual discoveries with our friends over coffee. In order for spirituality to be a genuine experience, to become an integral part of our lives, we must invest a measure of ourselves in a journey of discovery. This is a personal journey that begins within us when we take an uncompromising look at our hearts and souls and put into practice the three tools of spirituality.

HONESTY

When I speak of honesty, I am not talking about cash register honesty, that is, being honest in business dealings, not financially cheating others and keeping straight books. I am talking about honesty with ourselves.

Make no mistake, this self examination is not easy since our learned tendency is to ignore what is too painful to face — to hide from the truth. Honesty with self is rare. Problems occur on this inner journey the moment we rationalize something we find within ourselves that offends us. When we rationalize, we are lying to ourselves. As a consequence, we require countless other deceptions to keep our first lie intact.

Most of us grow up in families of secrets. I am sure if you are Irish like me you'll recognize the saying that secrets are a family's heirlooms. When I was growing up, there was much more we didn't talk about than what we did talk about. I was reared believing if I didn't think and talk about a problem, or if I wasn't honest in facing an uncomfortable situation, it would simply go away. Too many of us grew up this way. The reality is that this approach always makes the problem or situation worse.

Relationships can be healthy only to the extent that people are honest about problems they have with themselves and with each other. Problems in our marriages and families that aren't addressed or are ignored become secrets. They become eggshells on which everyone must avoid walking. The truth is that any family with secrets is a dysfunctional family, as is any marriage with secrets.

Recently, I spent a week with a couple who had done an extraordinary job of parenting. As is often the case I learned more from them than they did from me. What I learned was that of all the qualities they sought to instill in their children the one these parents most stressed was honesty with self. They didn't let the children get away with rationalizing, blaming others, making excuses, or finding scapegoats for their mistakes.

It wasn't easy for them. There were painful struggles as the children experienced the ache of love's first heartbreak and the sadness and disappointment of broken relationships, but by stressing honesty with self these parents were able to help their children process these life experiences, not bury them.

In over thirty years of counseling and preparing people to marry, I have learned that the most important quality one should look for in a potential life partner is honesty with self. You never know when you might need this information. I recently married a couple where the woman was eighty-seven and the man ninety-one. Even at their ages they still needed to look for personal honesty. Our society has shown itself adept at producing persons unprepared for marriage. I've counseled many couples where the woman is insecure and emotionally tied to her need for a man, while the man is emotionally bound up inside, angry, and unable to release that anger.

A relationship can overcome these difficulties as long as each is aware of and is honest about his or her problems. A woman who is insecure and emotionally tied to her need for a man can successfully marry if she is honest about how insecure she is; otherwise, she will always make the man the issue. A man who is emotionally crippled can also successfully marry if he is honest about it. If he isn't honest, he will always tell his wife that she is too emotional. If either partner feels a problem is not his or hers, it can never be resolved.

Let me illustrate how this concept of honesty with self works. Consider listening, with or without an agenda. Listening without an agenda means I don't have the answer before you start talking. I'm not already planning what I'm going to say next. Not only am I listening to your words but also to the feelings behind the words. I don't know what I'm going to say until after I've listened and genuinely heard. By doing this I can become someone who is not an expert, but a mentor, not a teller but a listener, not an authority but a companion on the journey. It is common in life to listen with an agenda. Listening with an agenda means I have the answer before I start listening. While a person is talking, I'm thinking about my response and how I want the person to whom I'm listening to respond to my response. We've all experienced it; we've all done it. Of course, that's not really listening at all. It's a method of control.

Imagine a clean sheet of paper. If I were to ask you to draw a picture of your face with your ears the size of the amount of real listening you do and your mouth the size of the amount of controlling you do, what would your picture look like? How honest can you be?

I often remind people that while God gave us two ears, he gave us only one mouth. My dad started losing his hearing about fifteen years ago. I often said to him in jest, "Hey dad, God took your hearing because you never used it anyway." I thought it was funny at the time, but now I'm losing my hearing, and it doesn't sound so humorous.

It is honesty with self that allows you to apply this to yourself. Only then can you change because if you can't apply this to yourself, it will go in one ear and out the other.

This is the kind of honesty with self I am talking about. It is the beginning of your spiritual journey.

OPENNESS

The second tool is openness. An open person is one who listens to his heart. Once we are open to God, we quickly realize that God speaks to us more through our own heart than through any person or institution. Our inner self is a greater source of truth than we will find anywhere outside of us.

Growing up in an alcoholic family, I learned this at a young age. My father was a bar drinker but still a very successful businessman. Later in life my dad found a spiritual program and remained sober for the last thirty-four years of his life. Though his sobriety was a great gift to our family, his heavy drinking during my formative years had a profound impact on everyone in the family. That impact, though, was one of our family secrets. When we attended church, all six of us — my parents and the four children — we would sit conspicuously in the front row. Everyone looked at us with admiration. "Oh, what a wonderful Catholic family!," they would say. It was common to be stopped on the street where people would comment, "Oh, if we could only have a family like yours!"

The reality was very different and even as a young boy I knew we weren't the model family everyone believed. Since my inner self told me that the perception we gave wasn't true, then I reasoned that perhaps many other things people said may not be true as well. From that early age I've never believed anything anybody said if it didn't make sense inside me. I've always listened to my inner voice.

As a consequence of this openness, the power people convey when they talk to me doesn't come from who they are or even what they say but from the reaction of my inner sense. Whatever we choose to call it — intuition or heart — that inner sense tells each one of us when we're around truth or falsehood.

This is how my ministry works. People often say to me, "When you said such and such I realized I had always known that truth. It had always been in my heart." I am not saying anything here that you don't already intuitively know. What I am doing by expressing it is giving you permission to believe what you have always known.

The problem is most people listen with their minds, not their hearts. The longest journey, I have learned, is from our head to our heart. Each of us to one extent or another is governed by a "committee" in our heads. This committee tells us how we ought to live — indeed, how we must live. Our parents are sitting on this committee. The people who taught us about God are sitting on this committee, as are nearly all authority figures from our lives.

The committee never changes since it was formed when we were youngsters, and with childlike logic it is uncompromising and unforgiving. While an open person is one who listens with his heart, a closed person is a person who listens through his committee.

As we travel the journey, we'll discover more and more the difference between the truths of the heart, of our inner sense, and the truths of our committee.

The consequences of this committee are far reaching and pervasive in most lives. Not long ago I was playing golf with a man I've known for many years. I'm not the world's greatest golfer so I'm happy when the ball simply goes forward. I joke that I play golf for Lent. My partner was the type who was shooting in the seventies, that is, playing great golf. Yet on every shot he complained. His shots were either too far to the left, too far to the right, too over, too under. He was driving me crazy because I was happy when my ball went into the sand or into the water as long as it was advancing.

Finally, at the seventh hole I turned and questioned him. "Jim, you're shooting a beautiful game of golf, but not once have I heard you give yourself a compliment. You criticize every shot you make. Why?"

Jim looked at me blankly at first. As we walked the course slowly his story came out. He told me that he grew up in a family with a father who never complemented him. He never heard, "Nice job, son. I'm really proud of you." His father always told him how he could do better. While it was true that Jim was playing excellent golf, it was also true that his father up in the committee was still judging his golf game, telling him he could do better. Jim didn't say if his father was alive or not, and as far as his committee was concerned, it didn't matter. His father sat in his head, noncompromising and critical.

When I wrote about listening with an agenda and listening without an agenda, who was the first person you thought of? Your spouse? Children? Parents? Or did you think about yourself?

In my ministry it's easy to become tired of hearing myself talk. There are days when I just don't want to speak because I am so sick of hearing the sound of my own voice, but I overcome this by drawing energy from the congregation that I am addressing. As I speak, I often see a wife or husband nudge their partner when I make a point, then lean over and say, "Did you get that?" They've been listening for the other person and I'll chuckle to myself.

The truth of the matter is none of us can change anybody into being the way we want them to be. Most marital difficulties center on this key issue. Just because we marry somebody doesn't mean we can change them. None of us possess that kind of power.

I've known many people who have made a marvelous mission — for their spouse. In Lancaster, California, a lady called me the second day I was there. She asked me to share her story so that others wouldn't repeat her mistake. She had persuaded her reluctant husband to attend the mission. On the way home from the first talk she said to him, "I sure hope you heard what father had to say." He never came back.

The greatest gift we can give to the people we love is to become the best person we can be. That's the only way we challenge other people to grow. We cannot demand or require another person's honesty and openness. We can only be open and honest with ourselves, allowing our own growth to create an environment that encourages the same to happen within others.

WILLINGNESS

The last tool is willingness. It brings to mind the expression, "After all is said and done, much more is said than done." We're a nation of great talkers, and too many of us don't know the difference between trying to do something and actually doing it. "Words are actions" is not only a modern political mantra but a way of life for too many. Well, words are not actions. Trying is when we're talking about it, and doing it is when we're doing it.

I have noticed something about people that remains consistent and allows me to know the size of my crowd at a mission before I start my first talk. If a number of parishioners say to me that they will try to attend, I know that I will have a small gathering. If they simply say they will be there, I know I will have a large crowd.

Wouldn't it be wonderful if by just talking about losing weight we'd actually trim down? When I started giving missions some years ago, I had a thirty-two inch waist and weighed one hundred seventy pounds. I backpacked eighty miles in the Sierras every summer and jogged forty minutes a day. I was in great shape for a man my age. After a few years on the road, experiencing different time zones, sitting for long hours at airports and eating in restaurants, I put on sixty pounds. From the moment I started gaining weight, I talked about losing it . . . and continued to pack on the pounds. No matter how much I talked about losing weight, I kept gaining it. You see, I wanted to eat sugars and fat more than I desired to lose weight. A few years ago I finally decided I wanted to lose weight more than I wanted to eat fats and I entered Overeaters Anonymous and willingly turned my fat over to God. I lost fifty pounds.

Indeed, I decided to deal with another addiction at the same time I first began to lose weight. I quit smoking. During the thirty years I smoked, I often talked about quitting but never did. In fact, I had quit many times, but I'd always ended up smoking again. The willingness simply wasn't there. I quit because doctors, family, and friends wanted me to quit, but I really didn't want to quit. The time finally came when I wanted to quit smoking more than I wanted to smoke. From that time on I've hated the smell of smoke. I discovered that to lose weight and stop smoking wasn't that difficult when I wanted to do these things, and made the effort.

I no longer do much marriage counseling because I have learned that both partners have to want to work at the marriage or I am wasting my effort. Now I meet separately with each person to see if they are genuinely willing to do what is necessary to make the marriage work. Only one of them isn't enough. If both don't commit, I don't counsel.

So much in life is determined by our choices, by what we want to do. Many people say, "Oh, I can't change. I'm too old, fat, tired, etc." What they're really saying is they don't want to change, and they're willing to use their age or whatever condition as an excuse.

We can examine our own willingness, or lack of it, by reflecting on how often we talk about what we would like to do and recognizing aspects of our lives where we've accomplished what we set out to do. We exemplify willingness when we accept the consequences of the choices we make rather than rationalizing or finding scapegoats.

This is no small step because it is through willingness that we're able to ignore and eventually fire members from the committee inside our mind. We can finally let go of anything in our lives that prevents us from experiencing the love of God within us.

These three tools of spirituality — honesty, openness, and willingness — unlock the gate of our inner spirituality. We cannot discover our spirituality unless we practice these tools.

Chapter Three

THE NEED TO BE PERFECT

3

A few years ago I read an article in the *Los Angeles Times* which reported that the new revision of the Catholic catechism was the first fundamental change in dogma for the Church since the 15th Century. This reinforced something I had observed for several years. When most of us were taught our religion, we learned a religion that was formulated in medieval times and was intended for medieval worshippers. Religious matters were explained to the people of the 15th Century in a way that they could understand. If you were sick today, would you go to a doctor practicing 15th Century medicine?

We are now moving away from that model. The term model connotes representation, image, a way of looking at something. It is obvious that the way people in the 1500's looked at the world is different from the way we look at the world today. Keep in mind that in turning away from these medieval teachings, we're not talking about the truth itself but rather how the truth has been explained to us, the model around which the eternal truth has been organized.

This change from a medieval to a contemporary model is not an easy one. This is going to remain a difficult problem for the Church for years to come because never before in recorded history has such a paradigm shift occurred within the span of a single generation. Adults such as myself were raised in one church yet live today in one that is fundamentally altered. Such a monumental change is unsettling for all of us. For example, I entered the seminary believing in one God, but I live today as a priest with a very different one.

I believe that many Christians still have a medieval notion of God, one that almost certainly stems from this model. A medievalist saw everything in terms of a spatial world, that is, they understood things by placing them in space. If something existed, then it must exist somewhere. So they put heaven up in the sky and hell down below. The soul was dark, white, or speckled. If we died, and it was dark, our soul went down to hell. If it was white, it went up to heaven. And if it was speckled, it went to purgatory.

Everything was viewed in physical realities. The power of good was depicted as an angel who was beside us. It was physical even though we couldn't see it. The power of evil was represented by the devil who was also unseen though still a physical presence.

Just as heaven had to exist in space, so did God. Therefore, God was placed up in the sky, in heaven — the eternal

Eye in the Sky, the Man upstairs, the Higher Power. God had a list of those who were going to die, a list of those who would recover from cancer, and those who wouldn't. I was born prematurely and spent my first two weeks in an incubator. I was even baptized in it because if I wasn't baptized and died, I'd go to limbo. That was how I got on the list to become a Jesuit because my mother promised God that if I lived, I would become a priest. You can tell how much medieval influence you have by the way you picture God. What do you see? Do you visualize a wise, old man with a beard surrounded by clouds? Is God a he or a she? When you think of angels, do they have wings? When you think of heaven, do you look to the sky?

Amidst the anguish and tears of my dad's passing, I was helped to believe in eternal life by reflecting on the love I had within me. This key insight helped me believe in a spiritual dimension, one that is much more real than the world we can see. As I watched my dad dying, I looked at my life and realized how I've always tried to be good; this realization is what kept me going and is what has kept me in my ministry. I understood that while we can't see love, it is as real as anything we can touch or feel.

From that experience I know today how much love is in me and that is my greatest motivator. The love inside of me is the most real part of me, but you can never touch it. It is more real than anything you see when you look at me. Once I understood that the spiritual kingdom doesn't exist in space, I was able to give my dad to God.

At a mission in Austin, Texas, a surgeon in his sixties approached me and said, "You just answered my own search for God. I know every part of the human body, but I always knew there was more to a person than just the parts I could see. For the first time I'm understanding what I have intuitively realized all my career."

Aren't we all much more than the parts of our body? Isn't our true essence something that an X-ray cannot detect? That core of our being is the love inside us, our personal experience with God. It is this kingdom within that Jesus came to bring.

Genesis says God created each one of us in God's image. The word "image" doesn't mean a statue or picture; it means personality. Through the act of creation all of us possess God's personality, this love within.

Every person I've ever known possesses the fundamental drive to love and to be loved. This comes personally from God. This desire to do good has come from the love that has always been with me.

WHY PERSONAL TURMOIL

The question then becomes this: If we possess God, then why are we in such turmoil? Why is there so little apparent love in the world?

One of the ways I answer this question is with this observation. People often ask me whether it's difficult to be a celibate priest, whether it's hard not to be married. The truth is that I don't see that many marriages I would consider happy or successful. Although I've seen some beautiful marriages, I haven't known that many so my honest answer is, "No."

In a sense I've chosen the easier way. It's less demanding to live a celibate life than it is to make a marriage work. Relationships are, by far, the most difficult challenge in our lives. Priests can administer the sacraments, counsel their parishioners, and visit the sick. They do this very well, but married people have to adjust to each other and to their children. In the process they're constantly surrendering some portion of themselves, and it exacts a toll on them and their relationships; however, it is also through this surrendering that they grow spiritually.

One way of dealing with these difficulties is to divorce. The desire to live in a relationship is a basic need for most of us, yet many don't know how to persevere so they move from one relationship to another. Many go through several marriages in their lifetime, a form of serial monogamy.

I've seen too few families where everyone loves and cares for each other, where everyone genuinely enjoys being around each other. One of the saddest things I've observed as a priest is the many people who are nicer to strangers than they are to their own families.

We live in a world of fast foods and over-committed agendas, and too many families today live as if they are wearing roller skates. Parents are constantly rushing and chaperoning their kids to some event or friend's house. Many families eat their meals while watching television. They don't sit at a table and have their meals together. They don't take the time to use the family meal as an opportunity to share the day's activities. Everyone is so busy running around, trying so hard, and nobody has enough time. Because of this fast pace we see the erosion of standards and civility.

A student once told me that her teacher asked the class to draw a picture of their families. In her drawing all the members of her family were holding hands. What she thought so common turned out to be the exception. Most of her fellow students had placed their family members apart, each in their own corner, occupied with their own interests.

These drawings sadly reflect the lack of cohesiveness within many of today's families. Instead of seeing themselves as part of a whole, many children view themselves as isolated units, each occupying their own space, without any feeling of family togetherness.

These reflections bring me back to the question I am often asked: Is love really possible? This question has persisted and intrigued me since I was a young man. What is the kind of love I have inside of me? Is it ever possible I will connect with another human being with unqualified love? I've concluded that it's the same as asking: Is God really possible? Because God is love.

We all ask this basic question, though in different ways. When we begin our search for love, we have in fact begun our search for God, though few people realize it.

I can only talk about God if there is at least one person I have loved without conditions and has loved me without conditions. This person can be a friend, spouse, parent, or soul mate who offers love with "no strings attached." I can't just talk about God and say the rosary, or come to the Eucharist, or quote from scripture; there has to be some experience of limitless love in my life. Why? Because God is love.

If God is love, and we all possess God, then I return to my first question: Why is there so little apparent love in this world? What are we doing wrong?

The answer lies in what has been handed down from generation to generation and how our culture reinforces it. In our time, in this culture, we've come to call conditional love, love.

CONDITIONAL LOVE

Conditional love is in fact not love at all. It's a device, and a very powerful one, for controlling others by making them feel guilty. "I'll love you when you're the way I want you to be, and I'll give you the silent treatment when you're not." There are a million ways to make people feel guilty so if it's not the silent treatment, there will be some other device.

This way of relating to other people comes from how we were taught about God as children. Some of us may not have been openly taught this way, but our parents likely were and subconsciously have passed the concept on.

Consider this for a moment. It is only natural that "we become the God we worship." We treat other people the way we believe God has treated us. We give away to others what is inside us. Therefore, all relationships are mirrors of our own relationship with ourselves and God.

As a child I was taught that God assigned to me an angel who maintained a list of everything I did wrong. They called it my good angel. I called it my tattletale. When I finally made it to the final judgment, the angel would read off everything on that list that I had done wrong. God didn't miss a thing. When I learned this, I remember thinking to myself that someday everyone would know all about me. This was reinforced by how I was taught about purgatory. There God was going to punish me for every wrong thing I had done. My mom still laughs about the day I came home in tears because I had learned from Sister Mary Veronica that even though I had confessed my sins, God was still going to punish me for them. I thought confession was punishment enough.

Let's examine the implication of these ideas. If God has a list of all the wrong I've done, if God is going to punish me for all the sinful acts I've committed, then God must expect me to be perfect. Right? Otherwise, why have the list? Why have the punishment?

The kind of God who expected me to be perfect was the same God who was going to punish me for what Adam and Eve did many years ago. That was spiritual abuse. When I was a child, I was taught that Adam and Eve's sin (the original sin) brought death and pain into the world. Someday I would get sick and die. If Adam and Eve had not sinned, I would never suffer pain or death. The good nuns taught me

I'd never have to go to school if Adam and Eve had not sinned since I would have been born with infused knowledge. I could have played my whole life. I hated school so I really resented Adam and Eve.

Reflect on this and consider its effect on a youngster. The God who expects us to be perfect is the same God who is still punishing us for what Adam and Eve did many years ago.

Since there's no such thing as a perfect family, we are all affected by this to some degree. Everybody I grew up with believed in this God. Since I was raised in an Irish Catholic neighborhood, all the friends I played with were Catholic. We all went to Catholic schools; it was considered a sin to go to a Protestant church. All of the people I grew up with — teachers, priests, nuns, family, and friends — were raised with this God who expected us to be perfect. The consequence was that we expected each other to be perfect. Whenever anyone did something wrong, the first thought was of punishment. After all, wasn't that the path God had shown us?

Recently, while I was giving a mission in Carmichael, California, a lady came to me angry about something I had done to her son twenty years before when I had been vice principal and prefect of discipline at the school he attended. Once she finished laying a guilt trip on me, I was about to become defensive in my response when I remembered what it was I had been preaching. "Ma'am," I said, "I'm sure I've made a lot of mistakes." She didn't know how to respond.

A society that expects everyone to be perfect creates inside us the desire to be perfect. We may know our faults, but it's painful to have others, our friends including our spouses, point them out. We don't like to hear about our shortcomings. We come to believe that the only way we can be loved and accepted is by being perfect. This way of thinking is so ingrained in many of us that we'll tell lies to others because we think if we tell them the truth, they may not like or accept us. This is why I believe it is so difficult to be honest with self. When we were kids we were loved conditionally. It was in these early years where we developed dishonesty with ourselves.

I remember that when I was in the second grade, I was placed in the hospital with an infection. During a visit my parents gave me a toy plastic duck to sit on the night stand beside my bed. That first day I inadvertently broke it. The next day my parents asked about it. I was so concerned they wouldn't love me if they knew I broke the duck, I said the nurse had broken it. It's the first lie I can remember telling.

I also remember a time during my high school years when my dad said, "Son, I know you're going to make mistakes, that's how we learn. Bad people don't learn from mistakes, good people do, but wise people learn from the mistakes of others. I don't care what you do, but always tell me the truth." It was a lecture he frequently gave all us kids when we were growing up. It sounded pretty good until one Friday night when I told him the truth and the roof came off the house. From that point on I was very careful about what I shared with my dad.

The price we pay for honesty is often too high, so we either lie or bury the truth. How many of us have lied because we think if we told the truth someone wouldn't like us? In relationships we frequently hear the question, "How can you lie to me? How come you're not telling me the truth?" However, the issue isn't truth or honesty but rather the price we pay for telling the truth.

There is a perverse consequence from all this deception. In pursuing this course with others, we inevitably lie to ourselves and thus deny ourselves even personal honesty. Ultimately, this is far more destructive than our external lies.

The real issue is love that is conditional and the pursuit of perfection based on conditional love. We attempt perfection by living up to other people's expectations. However, we can never achieve perfection because we can never live up to others' expectations.

Most parents do the best they can, but the expectation of earned love is passed from generation to generation and is a powerful, unconscious force. The way parents were raised is the way they tend to raise their children, and if there is no insight and growth in their lives, then that's the way their children will raise their children and so it continues.

As children our parents were our gods and this set the whole notion of God for us. We would do anything to be loved by them. Think back to our childhood. When we did something wrong, made a mistake — when we weren't perfect — were our parents there to help us grow and learn from it, or were they there to make us feel even more guilty? Were we more concerned about growing from the experience or more fearful of our parents' reaction?

That's the difference between conditional love and unconditional love. Parents, friends and spouses don't have to yell and scream to make us feel guilty. "How can you do that to me after all I've done for you?" Even without this stimulus we carry enough guilt ourselves.

When we hurt others, we feel terrible. Is the other person there to lift us up or to make us feel guilty? A moment like this is the precise point in a marriage, or any relationship, when we build bridges of friendship or walls of separation. In the case of a child, it is in these moments when we decide if we can trust our parents. I know people in their forties and fifties today who can open up to their friends but not to their parents. The term "intimacy" comes from the Latin word intertimeor, to work through fear. We can never trust anyone if we're afraid of their reaction.

Even today in our adult relationships, we can always tell when we're around conditional love because we're more afraid of the other person's reaction than we are about growing from an experience.

If we have already given ourselves the gift of a God of love, then our response to someone who has hurt us is instinctive, but if we haven't given ourselves this gift and are punishing ourselves, then we will punish others for what they do.

When a child is raised with conditional love, that child develops on the outside in order to please their parents, while ignoring the inside. Their parents thus become their personal experience of Adam and Eve. They will spend their whole life seeking their meaning in the person they marry, in their children, in their lifestyle, or their career. Those who attempt to find their meaning on the outside always measure themselves against another's list of expectations or criteria. I have spent my whole life worrying about whether you liked me or not; I was never concerned about liking myself.

I believe co-dependency is the modern word for describing this phenomenon; it is today's psychological term for original sin. When we are co-dependent, we seek meaning on the outside.

SHOWING US THE WAY

God has a response to original sin. That response is Jesus Christ, the Word made flesh. It is within this context of conditional love, our need to be perfect, that the story of Jesus Christ can bring a new and powerful meaning into our lives.

Anyone who has ever read the scriptures has to be overwhelmed by how painful his life was. He was born in a stable and died on a cross. When he was a boy, Jesus was taught to honor the priests, the Levites, the Pharisees; the respectable people in society. Yet they ultimately became his enemies and eventually plotted his death. He spent three years teaching his apostles that his kingdom was a spiritual kingdom, a kingdom within us, yet shortly before he died, they wanted to make him an external king, the Messiah who would drive out the Romans. He spent three years with these men, and they still missed the point.

You may remember Socrates, the great Greek philosopher, who was condemned to death for corrupting the youth. When he was condemned to die, he shared his wisdom with his followers concerning the immortality of man. He went to his death, surrounded by friends, in complete serenity and peace.

When Jesus discovered he was about to die, he endured deep anguish. Jesus begged his apostles to share this difficult time with him, but they fell asleep and left him alone. Twice he pleaded, "Father, take this cup from me," but it was not to be. It was only after the agony in the garden that he came to accept the Father's will.

One might expect Jesus to be more like Socrates, but it is Paul who gives us insight into Jesus. "Jesus became weak so that in our own weaknesses, we could learn how to become strong." That's what is mean by the incarnation, the Word made flesh. Jesus became human to show us the way to God. Jesus did it that way not because he needed it for himself, but because that's our path to God.

Therefore, the meaning of Jesus lies in the way he dealt with his brokenness. Whenever Jesus suffered, whether he was in the garden, the desert, or on the lake, he went to that love inside for his strength. Since he always went to that love, he discovered that it was always there; it was unconditional. Therefore, in the midst of his own journey, Jesus discovered his mission was to communicate to each one of us how much love is within us. We sometimes go to that love; Jesus always went to that love. He called that love "Father." Jesus could have called it "Mother," "Brother," "Sister," or "Friend," but he lived in a patriarchal culture where the love of the father for his family was the universal expression and example of unconditional love. The people who listened to Jesus were people who were broken, people who were in pain. He came in part for the lepers. In our time the lepers have become our AIDS victims, the people nobody wants to touch. He also came for the winos, the prostitutes, the elderly, the sick and broken, and those are with us still.

We don't find God through perfection or success since these merely satisfy our egos. Rather we find God through our imperfections, our failures, our losses. We must experience the "cross" to get to the "resurrection." We have to go through the "desert" to reach the "promised land."

God doesn't sit in the sky and plan all of this for us. Life is painful of itself, not because God makes it tough. Yet we still struggle on our individual journeys because we are looking for our meaning on the outside, having been conditioned to do so since childhood.

We spend much of our lives searching for the meaning of our existence, and we make into our god whoever or whatever we think gives us that meaning. The point of our life is not, as our media culture would suggest, entertainment, comfort, and pleasure. We all search for intimacy with God, but most often we are looking for it in the wrong places.

Some of us think we married a "god" on our wedding day. There is a great deal of pain in discovering that we didn't marry a god. Many people make their children god, and there is pain in discovery that isn't true. Many parents don't develop real spirituality until their children become teenagers or young adults. Some try to find god in their job or careers. Others have equated their god with lifestyle. Power, prestige, wealth, the country club, the shopping mall, and social committees can become gods in our lives. Over time there is a great deal of pain in discovering that our careers, wealth, and power bring us no meaningful satisfaction.

I recently held a retreat for a gathering of retired nuns. I asked myself, "What can I tell retired nuns? They should be giving me a retreat." What I learned was that for years their work had been their meaning, and now without that work they were faced with redefining their relationship with God. Here in the final years of their life, after a lifetime of commitment and dedication, they were just beginning to trust in God's unconditional love. They aren't alone. Many people don't find their God until they retire.

I think of my dear mom whose purpose in life for fifty-four years was to take care of my dad. Now without him she too must redefine what brings her a sense of worth, and it has been painful for her to take those first steps. Many people don't discover their God until their spouse dies.

In my life there has been pain in discovering the institutional church wasn't god and even more pain in realizing that being a Jesuit wasn't a god. I've spent half my life on my own cross. I have learned, however, it's while we're in that pain that we discover our personal God.

It signifies a special grace when we begin to realize that what makes us so precious is not our looks, our personality, what we own, what we do, or the people who love us. What makes us so special is the love inside us. Jesus points his finger back at us. "Look within and find the answer," he says. "The kingdom is within." We are "saved" from having to find the kingdom on the outside.

It doesn't matter when we find this special moment of grace in our life. What counts is that we begin the spiritual journey. When we understand this, we have accepted the good news of Jesus Christ.

I am reminded of the parable of the man who hired workers at the fourth, sixth, eighth, and twelfth hour of the day. At the end of the day he paid them all the same. This makes no sense if we consider the story in terms of marketplace economics. The point of the parable is that it doesn't matter when we make our discovery, whether we are 40, 60, 80 or 120; what matters is that at some time we do make that discovery.

It has been my experience, however, that we don't start to look within ourselves until we hit the rocks, until we've bottomed out. That happens because we've misplaced our identity into something outside ourselves.

49

We Christians have often confused the message of Jesus. I could go to all the Catholic shrines in the world, from Lourdes to Fatima, I could receive the Eucharist every day and have a great devotion to Mary, but all these things mean nothing if I don't believe I'm precious because of God's love inside. The message of Jesus is that we find God in the kingdom within. We can't love others until we love ourselves, and we love ourselves only when we let God love us.

ACCEPTING GOD'S LOVE

There was a man who taught me this lesson about letting God love us. He was, perhaps, the most successful man I've ever known. He owned the land upon which were built vast housing developments. He was tremendously wealthy and was the most generous person I've ever known. I could tell him about a poor family, and he wouldn't just give me a check or money. He would go to meet them, take them to the store, or to the doctor. He would share himself as well as his wealth.

Summertime in Phoenix is unbearable. Humidity in other areas is nothing compared to the heat in Phoenix. With all the irrigation, the pollution, the concrete jungle, and swimming pools, every summer becomes more miserable — four straight months of it. The people who were the most miserable in our parish were those living on fixed incomes because they could not afford to run their air conditioning. The only way for them to stay cool was through an evaporative cooler. However, during August, the humidity would rise, and with humidity these evaporative coolers didn't work very well.

I remember I used to visit these elderly people and bring them communion in their homes. I could never understand how they could endure cooking in their little apartments during the summer. This man, my friend, would find out who these people were and pay their electric bills anonymously. I don't think there's any greater earthly gift you can give anybody than air conditioning in the desert summer. He was, as I've said, a marvelous man.

But even he had one problem. He had always been self-sufficient. He would do anything in the world for anybody else, but he would never let others do anything for him. He knew how to give, but he didn't know how to receive. He refused to accept so much as a compliment.

He was a marvelous Irish Catholic. Every morning he attended 6:15 mass and would say the rosary before he went to bed at night. Tears would come to his eyes when he would talk about how much he loved God.

But there was a profound problem in his life. He didn't think God liked him all that much. He didn't give himself credit for being a good person, and as a consequence he carried within him a great burden of guilt and shame from his past.

My friend became terminally ill with cancer of the esophagus. When he died, he weighed little more than 100 pounds. However, the last four months of his marriage were the happiest period in his married life. Why? It was the first time he ever really needed his wife. He had always been self-sufficient, but finally, at the end she had to carry him to the bathtub to bathe him. He had become vulnerable and the circumstances compelled him to accept the love of another.

I was at his bedside the night before he died, and it was the first time in his life that he really let God love him. For the first time he gave himself credit for being a good person. He trusted God with all of his past. In those hours before his death, he recognized the love that had always existed inside himself and let God love him.

The experience moved me deeply. I'll never forget driving home that night pleading with God, "Please, don't let me wait until my deathbed. Don't let me wait to get a terrible cancer before I discover the difference between loving you and letting you love me."

This story illustrates how all of us can love God. Going to church, raising our children Catholic, or giving to the poor may be ways of loving God, but that's us doing it. Letting

God love us is letting <u>God</u> do it . . . believing we're precious because of the love that's within us.

If God's love is in us, and we believe it, then we must believe we are precious. We'll believe it when we approach the people we love, and instead of thinking, "Boy, am I lucky to know you!" we look them in the eye and think, "Boy, are you lucky to know me!"

In his gospel St. John says there is only one sin a Christian can commit. That sin is to refuse to accept God's love. It is when we choose to live in darkness. We do this when we belittle ourselves, put ourselves down, and treat ourselves as junk.

God's will is that we let God love us. It is when we choose to live in the light. We are living in the light when we believe deep inside that we are precious and special. It's God's love that makes us a special person. In refusing this love we behave badly, and traditionally it is those bad acts that are labeled as sin. Don't misunderstand me. I am not condoning bad behavior. It is to be condemned and avoided. But the sin is not the conduct; the sin is refusing to live in the light. To do God's will is to let God love us, and in so doing we find the happiness that lies deep inside us.

Psychologists tell us that we always reveal what's inside of us, one way or another. If we truly believe we are precious, we will do precious things. If we believe we are junk inside, we will do junky things.

To live in the light is to feel we're precious; to believe in ourselves, and to really like ourselves. St. John says that God's will is that we let God love us. All of us need to ask ourselves from time to time whether we're living in light or living in darkness. When we live in the light a new beginning awaits us, one where joy and meaning come from the inside. The good news of Jesus Christ is to bring us to God's love, to experience this kingdom of God within.

Chapter Four

SURRENDERING

4

Letting God love us sounds good on paper. Equating God's love with self love is usually met with a conceptual nod of agreement. However, truly believing in our own preciousness and embracing it in our hearts is another matter altogether. The longest journey in the world, as I've said, is from the head to the heart.

The difference between loving God and letting God love us sounds simple, but integrating it as part of our lifestyle is difficult because of our need to control others. It's much easier to love God, because we're the ones doing it, we're the ones setting the boundaries. When we accept God's unconditional love for us, it is a force over which we have no control.

Life is a process of surrendering. I have certainly found that to be the case. As an example, it's a common tendency for us to think when we get married, we'll change our partner. We may not speak it aloud, but deep within we believe we can change him or her after being together for a while. Because of this there is a struggle for control throughout the marriage as we repeatedly try to change our spouse, the partner we promised to accept "for better or for worse." Not long ago, I was driving to work and I heard a woman on the radio talk about her relationship with her husband. She bragged, "I'm in control of my man!" It's a common practice in relationships, but ultimately it never works. We'll make our lives miserable because we can never really change another person. They will never become the individuals we want. If the relationships are to prosper, we must let go and accept our spouses the way he or she is.

Parents do the same thing with their children. They try to control them; they try to mold them. Some parents have their children's future completely planned. However, somewhere in the middle of adolescence they throw up their arms and say, "God, you take over. I give up!" They let go because they must. Life, as I said, is a process of surrender.

I am fifty-six years of age at the time of this writing and have just begun experiencing an interesting metamorphosis. During the first half of my life, I essentially built up my own ego. However, in the second half, life has taken it down, a notch at a time. Life, I've learned, is surrender. We delude ourselves in thinking that we're in control.

Surrendering is difficult because we hate to give up anything. Just look at our closets and storage rooms. I recall a time several years ago after I had given up drinking, smoking, and eating sweets. I thought I was going to die of boredom. I went to see my doctor and said, "Look, I don't drink. I don't smoke. I don't eat sweets. I don't even have sex. I'm a celibate. Am I going to live to be 100?" The doctor looked at me and said, "No, Tom, but it's sure going to seem like it."

If we really want to believe in our own preciousness, to experience and practice unconditional love, we must begin by relinquishing two things — our god of punishment and our futile attempts to be perfect. Like old friends, they're inseparable and difficult to surrender. We must put a lot of willingness into this because it is easier to talk and read about than it is to do. There are two attitudes that through self-examination will prove helpful in learning to surrender.

LEARNING TO SURRENDER

The first is to recognize the mistaken belief that we're responsible for the happiness of others.

I mentioned earlier that I am the oldest in an alcoholic family. At an early age I became my father's father, that is, I became responsible for my father. When I later joined the Jesuits, I became a professional rescuer. I was driven by the need to be needed, the need to rescue. If there was a rescuer's Hall of Fame, my picture would decorate the entrance way.

When I was a priest in Phoenix, I was like *Superman* flying over the city, looking for the most troubled person around, and whenever I'd find one, I'd swoop down to the rescue. One of the hardest lessons I've learned in life is that I don't have the power to save anyone.

The only person I can make happy, the only person I can really rescue, the only person I can do it for is myself. No matter how much I love or care for another, I can't do it for them. Happy marriages occur not because the partners make each other happy, but because each partner has found inner happiness and shares it with the other. However, one partner can never make it happen for the other.

Many of us have experienced the loneliness and depression that overcomes us at certain crossroads. While there may be an individual who can offer words of comfort and friendship at just the right time, that person cannot rescue us. When we're in the midst of troubled waters, there may be others who will reassure us that we'll be safe, but they can't put us in their boat and pilot us to shore. We have to find the strength and courage to navigate our own way through rough seas and trust that God will guide others on their journey.

This is particularly true in raising a family. Parenting is, perhaps, the greatest challenge of our lives. As we raise our children, it is important we realize that they are only guests in our home. Their stay with us is a temporary one. Each one of them will have to go out someday and discover their own truths, each in their own way. No matter how much we love our children, we can't do this for them.

It's a common experience for parents to feel guilt because a child didn't turn out the way they expected or in a way that is socially acceptable. They often feel it's their fault when their children get a divorce, when they don't attend church anymore, if they fall into substance abuse, or live off society. What's the first thing that parents say? "Where did I go wrong?"

A good example of letting go is that during one of my missions I had the good fortune to meet a priest who was the most liberated pastor I've ever known. Although he was nearly seventy years old and had a very large parish, he seemed so free. He did something with his parish I'd never seen before and which I'll never forget. For two straight weeks he placed pads and pencils in the pews and instructed his parishioners to imagine the kind of parish they wanted to have in five years and what kinds of needs they wanted their parish to fulfill. Then he formed committees and told them it was their job to implement it.

"You gave the parish to the parishioners," I told him. "I've never known any priest to do that."

He smiled and said in a calm tone, "Tom, I've learned through my prayers that I'm not responsible for the parishioners' spirituality. They're responsible for it. My job is to serve as a facilitator."

I've known many priests who have burned themselves out by holding themselves responsible for their parishioners and attempting to control everything. In speaking to this priest I realized that I had spent much of my life trying to take care of everybody, and in doing so I had avoided taking care of myself. It was my cop-out for taking responsibility for myself, a way to avoid confronting my own issues. It was always much easier to concern myself with others.

We must learn to accept that we can't spend our lives tending to the needs of others. We can't put all of our energy into trying to make other people happy. We are responsible only for our own happiness, and when we have it, then we give it away to others. This single change in attitude can simplify our lives if we understand it and believe it in our heart.

The second attitude is what we focus on when we see ourselves. In the past when I got up in the morning and took that first trip to the mirror, all I saw were my mistakes, weaknesses, and failures. Throughout most of my life I never beheld my own preciousness. Now, I understand the reason why.

Many people from my generation and my parents' generation come from families where parents, especially their fathers, practiced silent praise. When we did something right, they didn't say a word, but they sure let us know when we did something wrong. When they were not saying anything, we were supposed to know that they were praising us — in other words, silent praise.

Many years ago I was giving a retreat to about eighty couples, including my parents. During the retreat I approached my dad and asked, "Do you think I'm getting as good as Father Barney?" Father Barney was a retreat master whom my dad liked and respected from the past. I wanted my dad to tell me I was doing a nice job and that he was proud of me, but he didn't say a word. Two weeks later he commented to my sister, "Hey, your brother's getting a big head. He thinks he's as good as Father Barney."

Throughout my life I had always allowed myself nothing more than silent praise. I never gave myself credit for how hard I tried. One day I realized if I ever knew anybody who tried as hard as I had, I would like and respect that person. I decided then and there to give myself credit for trying to live a good life.

During the sacrament of reconciliation I hear many people go through their laundry list of sins, and I'll think it's Al

Capone on the other side. Then I'll ask them if they've tried to be the best person they could be? Most people will say, "Father, I've sure tried, but I haven't been perfect." That's when I'll respond, "Why don't you start giving yourself credit for being the good person that you are?"

My dad and I represent in part a battle of generations. When he was a child, he was taught to look in the mirror and say, "I'm the problem." I've turned that on its head. I now look in the mirror and say, "I'm precious to God. The solution to problems I must face is within." In other words, if God's love is within us, we're precious to God and have worth. We praise God when we acknowledge God's love within.

LOVING OURSELVES

I have learned that an important part of my ministry is to give people permission to let go of old ideas. The question is always: Are they willing?

It's easy to be a Catholic, Episcopalian, or Methodist. It's not so easy to be a Christian. What determines whether we're spiritual Christians or not depends upon the kind of relationship we have with ourselves.

We've all endured individuals who put conditions on us and in so doing held us hostage. Conversely, there have been people who have loved and accepted us as we are. They are the ones we enjoy being with because we can be ourselves and we feel safe around them. It is easy to tell them the truth.

Of these two different kinds of people, which one are we to ourselves? Are we our own best friend? Are we patient, compassionate, and forgiving of ourselves? When we're having one of those screwy days, do we make it easier or more difficult on ourselves?

People become our friends when they support us during the times we're miserable and down. We trust them because they don't make the situation worse. How do we treat ourselves in moments like that? Do we get mad at ourselves when we fail, even though we know in our heart we've done our best?

So I ask: Are we our own best friend, or our own worst enemy?

Being human we will always make mistakes. Again and again, there will be situations in life over which we have no control, and the way we tolerate or resolve them is a reflection of the kind of relationship we have with ourselves.

I recall a time I tried to get out of Minnesota during one of the worst snowstorms in the state's history. Twenty-six inches of snow had fallen in twenty-four hours. My friends had arranged a large welcoming celebration for me at a beautiful parish in northern California. I knew if I didn't get out on Friday, I would be stuck and miss the event. This required that I drive one hundred miles through a rural section of the state to reach the airport.

Now I'm from San Francisco, and I wasn't used to driving in snow. When I started along the freeway at 6:30 in the morning, there wasn't a car in sight, and snow was blowing in every direction. I was afraid to take my eyes off the road to adjust the defroster so the windshield quickly froze up. Through a tiny, clear section of the windshield, I strained to see the road ahead of me. I thought to myself, "I can't keep going; this isn't going to work."

I took an exit and then found myself stuck in a snow bank. All kinds of angry and frightening thoughts raced through my mind. However, I settled down and said to myself, "Tom, stay calm." I realized that if I were driving with my best friend, I'd be there to calm him down and make it easier for him. That's what I did with myself. "I'll get through this," I said. "If I don't make it today, it's not meant to be. Don't worry about it."

Not long after this I discovered my car had front-wheel drive and I figured out how to use the defroster. I managed to get out of the snow bank, then hugged a big truck down the highway, and made it to the airport in time to take my flight back home. In the old days I would have yelled and screamed at myself for getting stuck, and probably would have remained in that snow bank until a tow truck found me.

Wherever we go or whatever we do, we bring with us either our best friend or our worst enemy because those are the kind of feelings we carry around inside ourselves. That is why so many people have a hard time being alone with themselves. When they walk into a room, they turn on the television. When they enter a car, they turn on the radio. They have to surround themselves with noise because they can't stand being alone.

The exact place where we decide if we are a Christian is in our relationship with ourselves. When we treat ourselves like we're special, we're accepting the good news of Jesus Christ. It is God's love within that makes us special. When we treat ourselves like our own worst enemy, treat ourselves like junk, we deny God's love inside us.

God is as close to us as we are to ourselves. When we lose ourselves we lose our God. When I look at the crucifix or make the sign of the cross today, I am reminded of how precious and special I am. Each of us is worth the life and death of Jesus Christ. This is the exact opposite of what I was taught as a child. Then when I looked at the crucifix I was reminded of how terrible I was because I had put Jesus on the cross.

LEARNING TO GROW

There is a tremendous difference between being self-centered and centered on self. To be self-centered means we have a dark hole inside, and we use people, places, and things to fill up that hole. To be centered on self means we make our relationship with ourselves our most important relationship. It is in this relationship where we find our personal God.

At the heart of who I am as a person is the good news of Jesus Christ. In centering on self I have had to make the two most important decisions of my life.

The first decision was to fire the god of punishment. For many years I had a profound problem as a priest. My favorite sermon topic was inevitably God's forgiveness; my problem was, I didn't practice it. I preached one God but lived another. I said wonderful things about God's goodness, love, and forgiveness. I thought it was true for the parishioners but not true for me. Whenever I did something wrong or failed, I would torment myself with guilt and want to disappear. I preached a God of love but I lived a god of punishment. My "committee" was standing in judgment. Rather than try to learn and grow from mistakes, I devoted my energy to berating myself.

Today I understand why I had such a god of punishment in my committee. I was not raised in a faith community, I was raised in a fear community. The priest then who did what I do today, evangelizing from parish to parish, preached a gospel of hell, fire, and damnation.

When I was in grade school, most of the good nuns had several stories to scare us with. Even when I was in high school, we had a Jesuit retreat master whose only job was to go to different high schools and terrify the students about going to hell. I was taught that a man could live a clean, beautiful life for eighty years; he could be a wonderful husband and father; he could go to church every Sunday and give to the poor; but if he committed one sin against chastity and did not confess it, he would go to hell for eternity. Missing mass once on Sunday or eating meat on Friday were sins against God and could result in our going to hell. Would a God of love do something like that? Would we ever do that to another human being if we were God?

I have noticed from my visits to retirement centers that as people get older they begin to "cram for the finals." They start looking over their past to see if there is something there that might prevent them from getting into heaven. On one occasion my dad's friend, who was eighty years old and dying from cancer, asked to see me. The man expressed his concern and remorse over stealing some sweatshirts when he was in high school. I thought to myself, "Here is a man

who is a great Christian, a great husband, a wonderful father, who is getting ready to meet his God, and he's worried
about what he did sixty-five years ago!"

What he shared with me was sad, for it illustrates the generations of men and women who suffer from guilt because
they have a god of punishment inside of them. While this
god of punishment may not be taught in the church today,
remnants of its effects are still a dynamic force in many
people's lives. This belief is passed on to their children —
and so it is passed from one generation to another.

One day I realized as an adult I could make my own decision about the God I would believe in. I could choose to
believe in the god of the bad news, as I was taught in my
youth, or in the God of the good news of Jesus Christ. I
fired that god of punishment and made a decision that from
then on I would have a God of love inside. That love would
be the directive force in my life.

I made the decision that from then on I would stop beating myself up and instead spend my energy growing from
experiences. This was the most important decision I've ever
made. This is one area that some of our Protestant brothers
and sisters understand better than we Catholics. I've been a
Catholic all my life, yet I was forty-five years of age before I
decided to believe in a God of love.

The church in which I was raised placed great emphasis on the sacraments which meant that important life events must happen in conjunction with the sacraments. Up until that time I thought I had made my decision about God when I was confirmed in the seventh grade or at the time of my ordination, but I realized that while I had been around religion all my life, I had never taken personal responsibility for my faith.

Faith is a decision, a response to God's grace of love inside of us, and we're only going to make this decision when we decide to do it. Nobody can make it for us. Reaching this decision to ground my faith in the love within me, not in some god in the sky, made my faith simple, though it didn't make it easy. I've done a lot of crazy things and made my share of mistakes; however, through it all I've tried hard to be good, to do the right thing. That desire to do good comes from the love of God inside me, and through it all God has never abandoned me. I've left God, but God has never left me.

After I made this decision, I didn't live in a rose garden. For a year and a half I had to make the commitment over and over. Whenever I did something wrong or unintentionally hurt somebody, I had to decide again whether I would grow from it or beat myself up.

Once I made this decision to focus on the love inside me, I noticed a profound turnabout in my life. When I changed my thinking, I changed my habits. When I changed my experience with God, I changed. When I used to beat myself up for doing wrong, I beat others up as well. I can't remember the last time that happened. When I grew from these experiences, my attitude toward others was to be there and to help them grow as well. All relationships I have discovered are mirrors of our relationship with ourselves and our God. We give away what's inside of us. This is how I made my faith simple, and since then it has become even simpler.

All of us commit some good acts and some bad acts, and in turn good things and bad things happen to us. However, it's not the event that makes us good or bad; it's whether we grow from the experience that causes it to be good or bad. Charity begins with who we are, and good deeds are a consequence that flow from this charity.

Sin is in not letting God love us. Not growing from something is refusing to let God love us. Sometimes allowing God to love us is simply making it through difficult times without becoming cynical or bitter. Sometimes it's becoming more compassionate toward others. Sometimes it's making us more honest with ourselves. Sometimes it means becoming more vulnerable towards others.

Most people make the mistake of beating themselves up over past events. As soon as something happens, the event is past — it is history. Yet these people are stuck looking back. What we must understand is that we can't change these past events, but we can grow from them. The sin is never the actual event; the sin is the process of not growing from our negative experiences. It's in not letting God's grace touch those events. It's in not letting God's love flow through our lives. Most outward behavior that we traditionally call sin is actually a symptom of what is happening inside us. We sin when we refuse to let God love us. The act may be very evil, but it only reflects on how evil the person feels about themselves.

I didn't learn this in catechism or theology. I learned it through my own pain and suffering. While I would never want to go through it again, I am grateful for these experiences and what they have taught me. If I didn't suffer all that pain, I would have never discovered the real me and what life is truly about. I would never have found a personal God. I had to go through the "desert" because that is the passage to the "promised land." We reach the "resurrection" by finding God's love while we're on our own personal "cross." That's how it works, and Jesus showed us the Way.

I've come to appreciate that some of the most beautiful people I've known in our parishes are the elderly. They are filled with goodness, love, and wisdom, and every line on their faces has a story to tell. They have been my teachers. As I came to know many of them during my years of parish work, I noticed all of them held something in common. They had all experienced pain, and it was while they were facing that pain that they discovered their faith. That's when they made their God personal.

Life is a journey; we never arrive. The whole purpose of our existence is to continue growing from whatever happens to us, from whatever hand we're dealt. The whole meaning of life is that we grow from our pains, struggles, and tragedies. We either grow from them or die with them, but we will never be the same because of them.

That's true for all of us. No matter what happens, we must keep growing. The good news of Jesus Christ is that God's love is always present; there is nothing that can happen in which God isn't present to take care of. What a difference it does make if on our journey we have with us a God of love. A God who helps us believe in our future rather than a god of punishment who makes us regret our past.

The second decision deals with perfectionism. Each one of us has difficulty accepting what I call our "humanness." We must learn to realize we're not perfect and never will be. We must make the decision to stop spending so much of our energy trying in vain to be perfect.

As I said earlier, some years ago I woke up one morning and thought of the many people I had come to know in my life. I had wonderful acquaintances and people who thought I was a wonderful person and a great priest. However, I realized there wasn't a single person who really loved me the way I needed to be loved. After thinking about this for a long time, I understood the reason why. It was because there wasn't a single person who really knew me. We can only love another person to the degree we know him.

It's not uncommon to experience in our parish, neighborhood, or work-place a person whom we don't like very much. Then one day that person shares something personal, and we begin to like him. This happens because for the first time we see them as they really are.

This brings to mind a personal experience a friend of mine related. Her friend Joe had recently remarried after being widowed for many years. He invited my friend to dinner to meet his new wife, Betty. She enjoyed the evening and was delighted that Joe seemed so happy and had someone to share his life with. However, she found Betty's face stony and her voice somewhat harsh. She was surprised that Joe had chosen her, but on the other hand, they seemed happy and compatible.

Several months later they had another occasion to share an evening together. They were discussing the O.J. Simpson trial and Betty commented that the verdict had gravely damaged the issue of spousal abuse. She then proceeded to reveal that she had previously been married to a batterer who had smashed her entire face. Her jaws were permanently wired and her cheeks had metal plates beneath the surface. Her broken nose and battered eyes also required surgery. She had to flee in the middle of the night to save her life. He would have killed her had she stayed.

This revelation from Betty caused my friend to view her with different eyes. No longer was she hard but a beautiful person who had suffered both physical and psychological trauma. Now the two of them are close friends.

I see this problem often in our marriages and in our culture with people who are unable to share themselves. Many men feel if they ever shared their vulnerabilities — their loneliness, fears, and anxieties — with their wives, their wives would fall apart. So they play the strong, silent type and wonder why their wives don't love them the way they need to beloved, never understanding that it's because their wives don't know them.

We live in a culture where businessmen and other professionals must maintain a <u>persona</u> of responsibility, of pretending to know the right answers, of exemplifying the company image. They don't dare talk about their loneliness, fears, or anger in a company environment, especially in these times when companies are downsizing. It's no wonder that so many of them flock to the bars for "happy hour" where a few drinks will help them unwind and where they often share with strangers what's really going on inside them.

We can only love somebody to the degree we know them. That was my problem. As the oldest in an alcoholic family, I always had to be responsible. Cemeteries are filled with men who die in their late forties and early fifties because of the stress of too much self-imposed responsibility. Responsible people can't say they're lonely, afraid, jealous, or angry because after all that's not being responsible. I had to be perfect and do things perfectly. Throughout my life I've had to give rationalizations and explanations. People used to say I had an answer for everything. At this point in my life, my hardest cross is that I'm still too responsible.

Today I'm learning how to become irresponsible. My personal motto is "anything worth doing is worth doing poorly" because if I think it's been done poorly, it's probably just about right. This doesn't seem to apply to many of today's young people, but it's certainly true of my generation.

I've been traveling around the country for more than a decade, and people often say that I look like an unmade bed. I never know how my hair looks or whether my shirt is tucked in evenly. Many times there will be a person who approaches me and will say that I remind them of Colombo. Inside I would think, "What do you mean? Don't I remind you of Robert Redford?" One day I decided it was time to watch the television series and find out about this Colombo character. What I discovered was that behind the trench coat

and old car was a man people liked and one they could identify with because he was human. I came to realize people
were telling me the strength of my message is that I'm human.

I had thought if people ever got to know me, they wouldn't
like what they found. I was wrong. Throughout my life I've
been around wonderful people, my family, friends, and the
Jesuits, but they all tried to change me to one extent or another. I felt there had to be something wrong with me because if I was OK, people would accept me the way I was.

I spent my life looking at myself under a microscope, worrying about my behavior, pondering how I could improve
it, how I could be better, how I could be . . . perfect. I thought
to myself that if I could be perfect, people would like me.
Now I've discovered it's only when people really get to know
me that they can come to love me.

A perfectionist can never find love nor be loved because
we can only love what's real. We can only want to love a
perfectionist. I thought being human was sinful, but being
human means accepting ourselves the way we are. My moment of insight came one day when I was preparing for the
sacrament of reconciliation. I realized that as I examined my
conscience, I was looking for all the areas that proved I wasn't
perfect (that I was human) so I could confess these to the
priest. It was then that I came to realize that my sin wasn't

that I was human but rather that I wanted to be god. I wanted to be in the Trinity: the Father, Son, Holy Spirit — and me.

So I decided to get out of the Trinity. I told people, "What you see is what you get." I decided not to change myself for anyone. The only thing I would change about myself would be my need to be perfect, and I had to be careful I didn't try to be imperfect perfectly. I had to let myself be perfect from time to time.

There are no words of scripture that have messed up my life more than all those sermons that exhorted me to be perfect as our Heavenly Father is perfect. Scripture scholars today tell us that the word "perfect" is an aeorist verb that means "to become," not "to be." It should read "to become perfected" as our Heavenly Father "is perfect." It means progress, not perfection.

We should be gentle with ourselves and accept the fact that we're going to have bad days, that we're going to do screwy things. If we ever expect to have intimacy in our lives, it starts with accepting ourselves. How can we expect others to like us if we don't like ourselves?

When we try to be perfect, we expect others around us to also be perfect and judge them when they are not. When we quit judging ourselves, we can start to accept other people and cease trying to change them. People love to be around people who accept them the way they are; people hate to be around people who are always trying to change them.

If I can do it, anybody can. I will put my humanness up against anyone's. I'm the most human person I've ever met. I was born compulsive. I've never done a moderate thing in my life. Even when I was a child, I went from one extreme to another. As a child before television, I had a bug collection. I couldn't sleep at night if I thought there was one more bug outside. When I got bored with the bugs, I started collecting tropical fish, followed by baseball cards. I wish I had them today.

Even now I can go from one hundred eighty pounds to two hundred twenty pounds in a month and nobody will see me eating. It must be my glands. When I'm staying at a rectory where the cook has baked a wonderful cake or pie for dessert, I will decline their offer of a piece with a polite, "No thanks. Too many calories." Then when everyone's asleep, I'm like Sherman's march to the sea. I'll eat every sweet available, nothing is safe. When I go to Tahoe, I play the poker slot machines. I even have witnesses who have seen me sit before the same machine for fourteen straight hours, while constantly drinking orange juice and coffee and never once going to the bathroom. It's a first class miracle.

I'm a sports addict. I've never enjoyed a 49ers game in my life. It's always a matter of life or death. One year when I was vice principal of a high school, we were playing for the basketball championship of northern California. Our team was behind by one point with twenty seconds left in the game. We called a time out, set the play, then called time in. Our side scored just at the buzzer, but the referee called charging and took the points away, and we lost the championship. There I was, out in the middle of the gymnasium floor, the dean of discipline for seven hundred boys, with my hands around the throat of the referee. I told you: I'll put my humanness against anyone's any day of the week.

GIFTS TO OURSELVES

There are three special gifts we can give ourselves that will emphasize our being human. If we practice them, they'll help us to accept and be comfortable with our ourselves.

The first is to allow ourselves to sometimes say, "I'm wrong." That's very different than saying, "I'm sorry," since being sorry doesn't necessarily mean I'm wrong. Remember that it's progress, not the attainment of perfection. Now I sometimes say I'm wrong, but for the first 45 years of my life I never once admitted I was wrong. I said I was sorry a billion times but thought the world would fall apart if I ever admitted I was wrong. God is never wrong.

It can be an amazing experience to tell someone we're wrong, someone who is used to us making excuses, blaming others, and rationalizing. When we say we're wrong, they look at us like we're speaking a foreign language.

Sometimes I have to practice saying the words, "I was wrong," in front of a mirror. That's how difficult I find them to utter. Rather than say these words most men admit they are wrong by no longer talking about the issue. How often have you heard, "I don't want to talk about it anymore!" In our culture it simply isn't natural for a man to say he is wrong. That's why he'll never stop to ask for directions when he's lost.

The reason why people always have to be right is because they must always be perfect; perfect people never allow themselves to be wrong. It is such a terrible tyranny. I've known too many people who would rather insist they are right and be miserable than admit they are wrong and be happy.

I once drove a woman home from the funeral of her husband. "Father," she said to me, "I loved my husband dearly, but in the fifty-two years we were married, I never once heard him admit he was wrong. You don't know how hard it was to live with him because of that." I answered, "Yes, but think how hard it was on him."

When we admit we're wrong, we grow from the experience. People who have to be right also have to be perfect. Perfect people can never be wrong, and that's a terrible burden to carry. It's not _who_ is right that matters, but _what_ is right that is important. What is right is that we love each other.

The second gift we give ourselves is to say, "I've changed my mind." This is especially important if we're people pleasers because we'll do or say yes to just about anything in order to make us feel good about ourselves.

In my case I can change my mind; what I have trouble saying is no. As a consequence, I'll work myself to death because when I work I feel wanted, needed. If you ever want anything done, ask someone's who's busy because they can't say no. Don't ask someone who's not busy because they have learned how to say no. One Christmas I went to six different Christmas dinners, and everyone thought it was the only dinner I was going to eat that day. I can tell some real horror stories about things I've done because of my inability to say no.

I've been a people pleaser all my life. There have been many occasions when I've over committed myself on projects and missions, where I've over scheduled too many appointments for one day. Rather than cancel any of them I would force myself to meet every commitment. This is still one of my crosses.

During the last ten years I have been on the road forty weeks a year, giving a mission each week in a different area. Someone will call and ask if I have a free week. I'll find one and agree to do another mission. I've learned to accept this about myself. I realize how difficult it is for me to say no so I've hired someone to say no for me. The crazy part is he isn't as responsible as I am. He forgets messages and doesn't return calls. But the end result is that I don't work every week anymore.

It is hard to be human. Let me show you why I often find it so hard to say I've changed my mind. Immediately after my dad died I was scheduled to do a two-week mission, and given my emotional state it would be difficult to fulfill this commitment. I called the parish director, explained my situation, and suggested we divide the mission into two one-week sessions to be held six months apart. That would give me the respite I needed at the time. She objected. The mission schedule had already been published, she said, and it would be very difficult to make the change I wanted. Now, I know the change could have been made easily, and given the reason — my dad's death — no one would have felt slighted. Instead, the director played her trump card. She said, "But you promised!" The irony in what happened next is that my dad, whose death was my reason for wanting the delay, had always taught me that you have to keep your word or you have no integrity. So I let guilt direct me and did the full two weeks.

My second example concerns a family situation. My dad had always promised my mom that after he retired, they would travel. For years she had never been beyond the bay area. But dad didn't retire until he was too sick to work so, of course, he was too sick to travel. After his death I took my mom to Yosemite and she loved it. She was eighty years old and had spent a lifetime in California; yet it was the first time that she had been there. Not long after that I rescheduled a mission so I could take her on a cruise. I explained my mom's situation to the parish director and said I was sorry, but because of my plans with her I had to delay the mission for a year. The parish director said, "I sure hope that my son will treat me the same way you treated your mom." When I hung up the telephone, I felt like a million dollars. She made me feel so human.

Life can be very difficult when we live around people who are always criticizing us and telling us how we can do something better. While it is so wonderful to live with people who love to be human.

Finally, the last gift we can give ourselves is to say, "I don't know." Thirty years ago my world was so black and white. Then I thought I had all the answers. Today I'm happy if I can just ask the right questions.

I know a man who left the Jesuit order shortly before his ordination. He started a company which prospered. Not long ago we met, and he complained that the young men he hired behaved as if they had all the answers. They were so sure of themselves. "Were we like that?" he asked. I laughed. My friend had been one of the worst in that area.

Several years ago I had dinner with three couples whom I have known for over thirty years. They asked me a question about the Our Father. "What does deliver us from evil mean?" they asked. I thought for a moment and replied, "I don't know." They all laughed because in all the years they had known me, they had never heard me say that. If I didn't have the answer I used to give a lengthy explanation using big words, and people wouldn't have a clue what I was talking about. It's so much easier to say, "I don't know."

One of the sad things in our culture today is that it's almost impossible for two men to discuss political issues they disagree on without becoming angry and personal. This is the way I look at it. There is at least fifty percent of our society that disagrees with me, and some of them are smarter than me. All of us have some of the truth; none of us has all the truth. If we listened to each other, we might start learning from each other.

When I'm around somebody who thinks they have all the answers, it tends to bring out the arrogance in me. Recently, I gave a mission at a parish whose pastor was an ultraconservative. At our evening meals I did my best to avoid a confrontation with him. By Wednesday night I had reached my limit listening to his pontificating. Finally I said, "Father, it must be nice to have all the answers. What I can't understand is why God is letting you hang around. Obviously you have nothing more to learn."

In contrast, my mom has taught me a lesson in growing old. She is for things; she is not against things. Often my mom and I are mistaken for husband and wife. Recently I went to a video store, and the lady there knew my name. "How did she know my name," I asked, since I had only been there a few times? She told me that she always remembered the nice people and that made me feel good. Then she went on to add that my wife came in the store often.

The difference in this philosophy between the old priest and my mom has taught me an important lesson in life. To be for something comes from love; to be against things comes from anger. There is no way a person can grow old faster than to be against things.

We don't have to know everything. Remember — we're not God.

The only way we're ever going to enjoy this life, to share God's love, and receive God's love from one another is when we allow ourselves to be and accept ourselves as human. As long as we try to be perfect, we're trying to be God. It will never work because we are not and can never be.

Chapter Five

FEAR VERSUS FAITH

5

Living is a daily challenge in which each of us struggles to balance the two worlds that vie for our attention. One is seen, the other unseen. One is finite, the other infinite. One lies beneath our feet, the other exists within our soul.

These two worlds, the material and the spiritual, coexist but cannot be treated with equal importance. One always emerges as dominant. Whether we realize it or not, by conscious or unconscious choice, the decision of which to emphasize is made every day and is manifested in the way we live.

We might consider which of these two worlds we have made a priority. Have we placed our primary concern in the spiritual or in the material dimension of our lives? Which is more important — the world of the spirit, all that is within, or the world of appearances, all that is viewed from the outside? Is it the person we share with others or the functions we perform? Which is more important — who we are or what we do? Where have we placed our faith? When we get out of bed each morning, do we strive to own, to possess, and to control; or do we live each day as a gift, one we'll never experience again?

MATERIAL VERSUS SPIRITUAL

I don't think there is a greater example of how these worlds are manifested in our lives than in the manner in which we celebrate Christmas. We know this holiday celebrates the birth of Jesus Christ and that its true meaning comes from our spirit of sharing, not in the gifts we buy. Yet immediately after Thanksgiving we begin to feel the pressure. The reality for many of us is that Christmas is characterized by struggling for parking spaces and fighting mobs at shopping malls. We often buy gifts more expensive than we can afford. We prepare for parties, fixing large meals while attempting to maintain a cheerful "holiday" attitude through it all.

Christmas is an economic hardship on most families. Parents are worried that their children won't experience a happy Christmas if there are not enough of the most popular presents under the tree. Media commentators tell us that Christmas will be successful or disappointing according to retail sales. Department stores litter their aisles with tree decorations, Santa Claus mats, and plastic figures of angels and Rudolph.

I'm not being Scrooge here. The smell of fresh pine along with the sound of Christmas carols and the sight of colored lights creates a certain enchantment. It can conjure up fond childhood memories. However, the emphasis on the material aspect of this season often buries its spiritual significance. Many of us express relief when Christmas is over, and I find this sad. Expressing our love through gifts is natural, but feeling pressured to do so is not.

The way we celebrate Christmas tells us a lot about our spirituality. Christians who try to live their lives with kindness, generosity, and compassion seize the Christmas season as an opportunity to celebrate how they live, but many others are so busy acquiring and possessing that they don't allow themselves to be Christians. When the Christmas season comes along, they attempt to compensate by buying expensive gifts for the ones they love. It never works. No matter how much money we spend we can never buy spiritual peace or attain intimacy.

The material world is neither good nor bad, and there is nothing wrong with having material possessions. It's wonderful to have a spacious home, a luxurious car, and be able to travel. However, the only way we will ever enjoy these gifts is if we've made the spiritual the primary focus of our life. The material should only celebrate and enhance the spiritual. It can never be a substitute for it.

Today we live in a culture where technology and the media permeate our physical and psychological lives. Beautiful homes and cars, large screen televisions with surround-sound audio systems, cellular phones, and megabyte computer systems have come to dominate our personal economic goals. The perceived need to possess these things has all too often resulted in both parents working. Day care centers are one of the fastest growing businesses in our culture. Radio, television, and the printed media routinely bombard our psyche telling us that the key to finding love and happiness is in a certain shampoo, an enticing perfume, or the fit of a pair of jeans.

From childhood through our adult lives we are constantly seduced into going to the outside for pleasure and fulfillment. So much of our time is absorbed in the material world that we lose sight of the spiritual dimension. Insidiously, and often without thought of the consequences, the material comes to dominate our lives.

Many of us work under the false concept of misplaced priorities. I worked at one parish where many young professionals — doctors, lawyers, and engineers — were climbing the social and economic ladder. These were apparently successful couples where both partners worked. On the surface they appeared to have every measure of financial success, but what I learned was that most of these couples were one paycheck away from bankruptcy. They were beholden to the material world, and it controlled their lives through the possessions they amassed.

Parents who have made a priority of their careers and neglected problems in their families cannot suddenly decide to reverse this cycle by "buying" family time. A once- or twice-a-year vacation, be it a ski trip or a week in Hawaii, cannot leave everyone feeling comfortable and happy. Life just doesn't work that way.

A friend of mine lives in Danville, a lovely area in northern California. He makes an enormous amount of money, but he has a family fraught with problems. He thought if he took his family on a cruise it would solve the family problems. When he came back from the trip, he called me up and said, "Tom, what a disaster, but what an expensive disaster!"

The eternal truth is that the material can never substitute for the spiritual. All of us know in our hearts that we can live in an ordinary house, drive a plain car, and be perfectly happy if we have love in our lives, but there's not a house nice enough nor a car fancy enough to satisfy us if we don't have that love.

PHYSICAL AS WELL AS MATERIAL

We not only live in a material world but also in a physical one. Just as the material can't replace the spiritual, neither can the physical. Perhaps one of the most intimate forms of expressing love to a spouse is through sexual intercourse.

Yet in my years of marriage counseling I've observed very few married couples growing in their sexual union. If they don't increase in trust and in their ability to communicate with one another, if they can't go out, laugh and play together, they have nothing to celebrate in a physical relationship.

The sexual can only enhance the spiritual; it can never substitute for it. If the sexual could do it, we'd be the happiest culture in the world. If a couple doesn't grow spiritually as individuals and together, the physical relationship soon loses its force and vitality.

MY FAITH

In the midst of the kind of society in which we live today it's very important that we question what we've chosen to make a priority in our lives, that in which we've placed our faith. We should take time to reflect and ask ourselves: In what do I really believe?

Let me share my faith, and I ask that you reflect on what it is that you have placed your faith. I was raised like most Catholics who are my age. I was reared to believe in a God who created me and one who would punish me, an impersonal God that performed functions. This kept me reasonably straight because I was scared of hell.

When I joined the Jesuits, life became more complicated, and I began experiencing adult problems. Because of my upbringing I believed in this God who performed functions, one who creates and judges. However, such a God isn't very personal, so when I needed a personal God I couldn't find one. For many years, even as a priest, I had little faith. I basically preached humanism, a gospel of how to live as a good human being.

I have an awfully simple faith today. My dad often said to me, "Son, if you don't keep it awfully simple, it's going to get simply awful." I didn't understand it then, but I sure do today.

GOD IS LOVE

I believe in the good news of Jesus Christ. For me it simply means God is love. Whenever I say the word God, I can also say the word love. I experience God on a personal level whenever I remember the love between my parents, the love within my family and friendships. I realize that this love inside of me has been there my whole life. I had been searching for it as the song says, *"In All The Wrong Places."*

Recently, a young man approached me, looked me in the eye, and said, "You really believe that God is love, don't you?" I told him if that wasn't true, then this whole world is absurd. It's the only thing that brings meaning to life.

97

Our most important drive in life has always been to love and be loved. This desire comes from the love inside us; it comes from God. That love is unconditional, always forgiving, and forever present. Nothing can happen to us that God won't be there to take care of. We'll never be alone. This is what the good news of Jesus Christ means to me.

My faith is important to me because the older I get the more I realize that "life is what happens while I'm making other plans." Let me give you some examples of what happened this last year. This year should have been my year off. I needed to take time from my rigorous schedule to recharge. My two coworkers are firemen and dependent upon my ministry to subsidize their income. Their family situation had changed as all their kids were now in school. Their wives could now help out with the family income. Such was my thinking. So I decided to go ahead and take the year off. Just as I began laying plans one of my coworkers told me he had unexpected news. "Tom, I think my wife is pregnant."

"Oh," I said. "That wasn't in our plans."

"Don't worry about it," he said, "It's probably a false alarm. She's seeing the doctor tomorrow."

The next day, a Wednesday, he called to say, " The doctor told us that she's pregnant." The next day he called back, " The doctor says it's triplets." There went the year!

In addition to my coworkers I also have a nonprofit corporation. Every summer my workload is light, but the bills don't take a vacation. Come September I had worked a long stretch to get caught up on my obligations. I had worked nine straight, hard weeks and had just completed a mission in Olympia, Washington. The bills were paid, there was inventory in the office, and money in the bank. I decided I had the time to take my mom to Lake Tahoe. I often tell my friends that I'd rather be miserable in Tahoe than happy anywhere else. I was packing the luggage when the telephone rang. It was one of the fireman informing me that our office had burned to the ground — and he had neglected to take out fire insurance! It cost me sixty thousand dollars to undo the damage. I used to preach that if you have a problem that money can solve, it's not a real problem. Health and the loss of a loved one is a problem. Let me tell you I learned that's a harder doctrine to live than it is to preach, but we eventually made it through and paid our bills.

Then I came home for Christmas with a month scheduled off, the longest in twelve years. I was planning to get outdoors, to go skiing in the recent snow. I was home for two days when my mom came down with hepatitis. I spent the month taking care of her, and I was glad to be there, but it wasn't a vacation. As I said, "Life is what happens while I'm making other plans."

No matter how much effort I put into someone or something, I can never be guaranteed that people or things will turn out my way. People who place their faith or their meaning in results, events, or persons are filled with fear because they place their faith in someone or something they cannot control. My faith exists no matter where I am or what I'm doing. God is with me. I have no idea what I'll be doing a year from now. I could be married to a woman with fifteen children. Ask anyone who knows me well, and they'll tell you that I'm impulsive enough not to notice the kids, but even if I married a woman with fifteen kids, God would be with me. God better be with me.

Or take another extreme. I could be dead. I recently attended a funeral for one of the stars of my high school football team. He was one of the most popular guys in the school and was the one the girls liked. Now he was dead. I've reached the age where I attend more funerals than I do weddings, but whatever happens, wherever I am, I know that God is with me.

Now comes the crux of the issue. I can live by either fear or faith. Today I have a choice. This is an area where we must be honest with ourselves. People must really ask themselves this question: How much of a controller are they? How much do they try to control their wives, their children?

If we want to understand how much of a controller we are, all we have to do is to appreciate to what extent fear runs our lives. It is fear that makes us control. Understand that control isn't giving advice, offering suggestions, or even delivering a lecture. Control is when we make others pay a price when they don't do what we want them to. My dad could give me a look that would send me into a two-week depression. That's control.

The people who most often need to hear about being a controller don't even know I'm talking about them. It is part of a strange phenomenon that often the people who most need to hear something don't even know it pertains to them. I am often approached during my missions and asked why don't I preach about hell, fire, and damnation. I tell them that I preach God's love; if they don't believe in this, they will create their own hell, fire, and damnation. What they most need to hear about is God's love because these people are the most rigid in their thinking and behavior; yet every time they hear about God's love they want to report me to the Bishop. So why is it that those who most need to hear this message, don't? I have found that if you lie enough to yourself, over the years you come to believe your own lies. The lies become your denial system.

To some extent we are all controllers since it is part of the human condition. This control sets the stage for anger. We become angry when people don't appreciate how much we're controlling them for their own good. We become angry when people don't behave the way we want them to. We become angry when events don't turn out as we think they should.

FEAR — CONTROL — ANGER

Fear - control - anger. Do any of us recognize the cycle? Those who don't are, often, in denial. I know, I used to live that way all the time. Today I have an option. I can live by fear, or I can live by faith. Let me share some examples of how I live by faith.

I was approached some years ago and was asked to do a television show, part of a PBS pilot series on spirituality. I realized that in one hour I would reach more people on television than I ever could working as I was. I was immediately consumed with ego and thought I would become famous, another Bishop Fulton Sheen. I wondered how I'd look in a cape. The week before the taping in Long Beach, California, I went to Atlanta, Georgia, to conduct a mission. When I travel, I stay in rectories, and when I entered this one, all the priests were sick with walking pneumonia. I always think if the worst can happen, it will happen to me. I became convinced I was going to become sick. The more you feed fear, the bigger it gets. I could envision the germs in the air coming after me. When I woke up one morning with a sore throat. I panicked and started popping vitamin C like candy; I even went to a doctor for a B12 shot, something I had never done before. I really wanted to tape the show. I wanted my splash of fame, I wanted to broaden my audience, and I feared my chance was slipping away. I was convinced I wouldn't be able to perform, especially since I had to fly cross-country the day before the talk.

Four days before the taping, while in Atlanta, I brought it to prayer and there I surrendered my fear. I accepted whatever was going to happen because I had faith that God's love was inside of me. Surrender is acceptance. I accept what happens, not because I like it but because I have faith that God is with me. The love within makes this possible. I wrestle with these moments for they are not easy. I don't just casually give it to God, but eventually I am able to say, "Be it done unto me according to Thy will."

Had I given into fear, I likely would have become sick since nothing makes us ill faster than stress. When it came time for the show, I was fine and I gave one of the best messages I have ever delivered. The audience gave me a standing ovation. Later I learned the show couldn't be used because the sound equipment was faulty. I decided it was not meant to be. I've known many people who have become famous and they thought they were better than others. This fame caused them severe personal problems and often ruined their lives. I decided that the best way for me to share my message is on the personal level, parish to parish.

In another example, while I was holding a mission I received a call informing me that my dad had suffered a heart attack. He was driving on the freeway when the car suddenly veered into the oncoming traffic. My mom looked over to see my dad behind the wheel with his head back and eyes open — dead. She grabbed the wheel to avoid the oncoming cars and after spinning around the car stopped. A truck driver behind them pulled off to the side, called the paramedics, then gave my dad mouth-to-mouth. He had been technically dead for several minutes, but the truck driver was able to revive him.

The real miracle, however, occurred when my mother, my two sisters, my brother and I came together in the small town of Novato, California. For four days we waited, hour by hour, not knowing whether my dad was going to survive. It was during that time we gave our father to God and accepted whatever was meant to be.

Those four days were the greatest experience of God, the greatest experience of love I've ever had. We were able to nurture, support, and care for each other. "What a difference faith makes," I thought to myself. I've seen families during times of crises when fear takes over and everybody turns inward and becomes wrapped up in their own insecurities. As a result, an unfortunate, tragic situation becomes even worse.

My dad survived and then had open heart surgery. His condition remained fragile for the remaining five years of his life. During that time I noticed that when my father accepted his condition, he was at peace and enjoyed living, but when dad fought it, those were the times he became depressed about dying.

Surrender is acceptance. We accept reality not because it is what we want or like, but because we have faith that God's love is with us. It's not easy. However, if I bring my fears to God, eventually I can say, "Be it done unto me, according to Thy will." I can let go because I have given it to God.

What we're releasing is fear and, in its stead, placing our trust in God. The only way we'll ever find and know inner peace is when we have faith that God is with us. This gives us the freedom to accept reality as it is; otherwise, we spend our lives fighting reality, filling it with ceaseless stress.

There is a very simple way to determine how spiritual people are: they are able to look at life and say that everything happened for a reason. This doesn't mean that everything was wonderful or that they'd want to go through it again but rather that they grew from the experiences. Growth became the reason it happened. If they didn't grow from it, then it didn't happen for a reason. If they grew from it, that meant they were committed to God.

The amazing thing about my journey is that the events for which I am most grateful were also my most painful. I wasn't grateful when I was experiencing them. I thought I was going through hell, but when I started growing spiritually, I could look back and be grateful.

If people can look back at their whole life and be grateful, then they don't have to be afraid of anything that might happen to them in the future. The good news of Jesus Christ is that the same God who was with them throughout their journey will be with them forever. There's not a thing that can happen to us that God won't be there to help.

FEAR OR FAITH

Another way to perceive how this spiritual process works is to think about how we look at ourselves. Do we consider ourselves a person first or a persona? In other words, do we define ourselves by what we do or who we are? We are meant to be human beings, not human doers.

We can always tell when we meet a real person because they're spontaneous and alive; they live from within. It is our faith in God's love that allows us to accept who we are and gives us the freedom to be ourselves. We can also tell when we've met a persona. We can know this persona for twenty years and never know them better than the first day we met them. They are not real.

If I find my meaning in who I am, then I'm a person first. If my meaning comes from what I do, then I'm a persona first. If we don't find meaning in who we are, then we'll attempt to find meaning in what we do. This will eventually create tension and stress and manifest itself through us as a persona.

I've been a Jesuit since I was seventeen years of age and a priest since I was thirty. I pray every day that I'm a person first before I'm a priest. I would be a very selfish man if I baptized children, buried the dead, and preached sermons, yet didn't share the greatest gift I had to give — the gift of myself. When people get to know me, I often hear them say, "I never knew you were a priest." I take that as a compliment because people are telling me I'm a person before I'm a priest.

This isn't always the case. Personas abound. There are some priests we could know for many years and yet never really know them. We'll know them only as Father. Instead of having found meaning in being themselves, they have found their meaning in being a priest. You could put them in a room with forty men and pick them out as priests.

I've known women who have the mothering persona. They mother their husbands, children, and everyone who comes into their lives. They may be wonderful mothers, but the greatest gift they have to give is not what they do for others, it's the gift of themselves. They've developed the mother persona because they find their meaning in being a mother, not in being themselves and allowing others to know them. I don't want my mom to do things for me; I want her to share herself with me.

When I was a young man making my first important decisions about life, I decided I wouldn't marry a woman from a culture where wives tended to mother their husbands. I didn't want to marry my mother because I already had one. I wasn't going to marry someone to take care of me but someone with whom I could share my life.

One of the most frustrating retreats I've ever given was a spirituality weekend for football coaches. During my best material they sat there like rocks. I think they were diagramming plays in their heads. During the break they strutted about the room like little Vince Lombardis. They derived their meaning in life from being a coach, not from being themselves. They even called each other "coach."

All we have to do is spend ten minutes with our doctor or lawyer and we'll know immediately whether he's a person first or a persona. I'm having my first experience with lawyers in dealing with my nonprofit corporation. As a Jesuit I've spent many years in the classroom. I've studied Hebrew,

Greek, Latin, French, and German. However, when I receive a document from my lawyer, I don't have a clue what it's saying. I'll even try to read it a second and third time and still won't have a clue. It would be nice to sit down and talk humanly with the lawyer about what's really going on without being charged another thousand dollars. Then when I get the bill, I need a psychiatrist to adjust. I've had the same experience with doctors.

When my dad underwent back surgery, the operation took four to five hours beyond what had been anticipated. Sitting in the waiting room all that time was difficult. When the doctor came in, he summarized what happened in one and a half minutes of jargon that not one of us understood. I've known doctors who have told patients they have six months to live with as much compassion as telling them to take two aspirin and call them in the morning.

It doesn't have to be like that. Several years later when my dad lay dying, the doctor who performed his open heart surgery twice dropped by the house to patiently answer our questions, give us advice, and make us feel like it was his privilege to be there.

If we're in pain, if we really need someone, it makes all the difference in the world if the person we go to — whether it be a doctor, lawyer, priest, or teacher — is a person rather than a persona. Defining ourselves by what we do only produces rigid, shallow relationships, whereas placing our value in who we are creates honest and fulfilling relationships.

ETERNAL LOVE

The author, Rollo May, maintains that one of the hardest days in a man's life is the death of his father, and one of the hardest days for a woman is the death of her mother. What makes that day either easier or harder depends upon whether we've ever become friends with our parents, because if we have, it's much easier to let go. However, if we haven't become friends, then we'll carry the pain of unresolved guilt for the rest of our lives.

When I first read that, it really frightened me because at the time I had a persona relationship with my father. He was my dad, and I was his son. It may have seemed that I had my life together; however, when I entered my parents' home, I reverted to being a fourteen-year-old. I spent all my energy trying to please my father, and he spent all his energy telling me how to please him. As an adult I would have dinner with my parents, and my dad would look at me and say, "Son, you're eating too fast." I would take him out for a drive and act as if I were in Driver's Ed. I was then in my forties and didn't need a father; he was in his seventies and didn't need a son. What we needed was to be friends.

Whenever I was around my dad, I used to feel terribly lonely because I could be myself around my friends, but I couldn't be that way around my dad. I'm sure he felt the same way. He was a strong, successful businessman, a self-made man who started out as a floor boy and had worked his way up to become the manager of one of the largest furniture companies in the country. I didn't know how to approach our relationship other than as father and son because I never knew what his reaction would be.

It was during a couple's retreat which my parents attended that I shared with the group my feelings about the stifling relationship I had with my dad. After that conference my dad and I began a new relationship. We went for a walk. We talked, hugged, cried, and shared things we had never shared before. You can't love anyone unless they let you know them.

For the first time my dad told me his story. He told me how his father had abandoned him and his mother when he was six months old. He shared with me how hard it was to grow up without a father and what his life was like during the Depression. He had to work two different jobs while attending grade school just to put food on the table. As he shared his story, I slowly began to understand him. It has been my experience that Depression Era men had to be dictators, had to be in charge. Tough times create tough men.

They had to be in charge at home as well. This was a conversation we never had in the home. My dad, I realized, was one of those men. If we were to talk, it would have to be away from the house. Our first walks together were the start of a beautiful friendship.

Following that breakthrough when I'd returned home to San Francisco to visit my parents, my dad and I would often take long walks around Lake Merced and share our lives with each other. These were our best times together.

During his last year we would spend Wednesdays together. One day I took my father to Watsonville south of San Francisco. This was where he had been born and I heard stories about his childhood that I really needed to hear. He shared so much about his life that I had never known. Shortly before his death, when dad knew he was dying, I took him to the delta, where he kept his boat, to say goodbye to his fishing buddies. I was deeply moved by this experience. Those times and the memory of them have meant much to me.

When I arrived at my dad's hospital bed and saw the tubes in him and machines surrounding him, I could hold him and know that he wasn't just my father; he was my friend. I knew that was one of the most important gifts God has ever given me.

ETERNAL LIFE

I believe that anyone who has discovered real love believes in eternal life. Whenever we really love someone, we want to love that person forever — not just for a day, a year, or even a lifetime. When two people truly love each other, they have special moments in their love when they experience God's presence. I refer to these as "moments of the divine." These moments of light may be few, but it's those times that keep people going during the dark times.

I have observed that people who live life the most fear death the least, and those who live life the least fear death the most. Our greatest fear in life should be that we will die without ever discovering God, without ever discovering love.

I believe the reason God created each of us is not to fulfill some agenda — to be married, to have children, or to be successful. It is to discover the love that is inside us and to share that love with the people God sends into our lives.

Once we experience that love we come to understand eternal life — that God is love. God can never die, and so love can never die. I believe that when God calls each one of us home, we'll be reunited with all the people we've loved and those who have loved us, and we'll live in that love forever. I'm not sharing this because of what I've been taught about eternal life but because this has been my experience of love.

One of the most meaningful events of my life was the death and burial of my father. I had presided over many funerals before then and shared many of the thoughts I just expressed, but I always wondered what would it be like when I had to bury one of my parents. It was painful; we would miss dad terribly. However, there was such an inner peace in our family that there was no deep depression or bitter gloom. There was inner joy, even some laughter because everyone in our family knew, each in his own way, that the kind of love that had come to exist in our family had to be forever. My sister recently told me she hasn't been afraid of death since we buried our dad.

Everything I believed about the Gospel was verified in my dad's death and burial. It brought real resurrection to our family. Nothing has ever done more to help my own faith in eternal life.

Let me share my experience of hell with you. It is the absence of this love in our lives. Hell is when we live as a persona and never discover that God is love. It is when we never risk ourselves with another. We remain spectators and observe life as it passes us by. When we die they put us in a coffin. There was nothing before, nothing during — and there is nothing after. What is hell but the absence of God, the absence of love?

Many of us become caught up in the material cycle without realizing it is an illusion. So many people become miserable as they grow older. Their children don't come around to see them, and they hardly know their grandchildren. They sit alone in their rocking chairs. All the money they have and the material things they own don't make them happy. They're miserable because there's no love in their life. They have created their own hell.

None of us ever become perfectly spiritual. We never completely get there. We live in a material world that we can't shed like a set of clothing. Every day we traverse our way through these two paths with the hope that we become more spiritual and less material.

It's progress, not perfection — process, not product — because life is a journey.

Chapter Six

OUR GREATEST FEARS

6

On my spiritual journey one of the prayers that has most helped me simplify my life is the prayer of contemplation. It challenges me to learn what it is that God is calling me to do.

With the lights off I lie down on my bed and quiet my body. I focus on my extremities, relaxing each until I am no longer aware of them. Then I slowly calm my heart and my breathing. I move methodically to every part of my body until I am as relaxed as possible. Then I ask God for the gift of honesty.

I ask myself to imagine I am dying right now; I make it as real as possible. Then I ask God what are my regrets? What are the things I wish I had done? The regrets and misgivings that come to mind are crucial because those are the situations and relationships that God is calling me to heal.

All of us tend to put things off until tomorrow, next week, or even next year. Yet, for each one of us there will come a day when there is no tomorrow. Wouldn't it be wonderful if on our death beds we could honestly say, "I have no regrets. I lived my life as best I could. Father, into your hands I commend my spirit." Wouldn't that be a wonderful, final grace?

Twelve years ago while I was offering this prayer, it dawned on me I had never as an adult told my mom that I loved her. I also realized that my mom had never spoken those words to me as an adult. Imagine the pain and regret if one of us had died and left those words unspoken.

I've mentioned that I grew up in an alcoholic home. Alcoholism is a disease that affects the whole family, not just the alcoholic. My dad frequented the Irish bars in San Francisco, and he would often stay out until two or three in the morning. While he would be having a marvelous time — singing with the guys, dancing on the table, having his own party — my mom would be at home, waiting for him. She was filled with loneliness, fear, and anger, suffering great pain. I often sat up with her and watched as she smoked one cigarette after another.

People who live with pain year after year eventually have all the emotion drained from their lives. This becomes apparent in their faces which may still reflect kindness, but all trace of emotion or natural expression has vanished. Such was the case in our family. We went through so much together, but we didn't know how to share our feelings.

It was during this simple prayer when I decided to tell my mom I loved her the next time we talked. I call her every Sunday and I'll never forget that conversation as long as I live. It started in the usual fashion. We're a sports family, so the first thing we talked about were the 49ers, the Giants, and the Golden State Warriors. Then we talked about California politics and the family news. It was a typical family conversation. When we reached the end of our weekly chat, I struggled with what I wanted to tell her. It was one of the most difficult sentences I've ever uttered. I finally managed to say, "Mom, I love you." All I could hear on the other end of the line were my mom's sobs. "Tommy, I love you so much," she said finally. That sentence opened the way to the development of a wonderful relationship.

Our families are the most important reality in our lives, yet often it's difficult to communicate our innermost feelings to them. This is because the people who matter the most to us are also the people with whom it's hardest to take risks. When my dad underwent open heart surgery, I was conducting a women's retreat. During his operation and three days of recovery, those serious days when so many things can go wrong, my family came together. Since the retreat site was only an hour drive from the hospital, I was traveling back and forth between the retreat and the hospital. When I finished the retreat on Sunday afternoon, I returned home and found my mom sitting in a chair in the corner of the living room. It was just the two of us. She looked exhausted and drained.

I said, "Mom, you're the most precious, special woman I have ever known. I've never known a woman who had so much love and goodness inside." Her eyes widened as I continued. "I've known a lot of women. In fact, I just finished with one hundred ten of them. Mom, I would tell you that even if you weren't my mother."

Tiny droplets of tears began to flow down her cheeks. "Tommy," she said to me, "you used to be so angry at me." She was right. I had been.

You see, for years I had blamed her for my dad's drinking. When he came home drunk, she'd give him the silent treatment, and he'd go out on a two-week binge. I always felt that if she didn't treat him like that, he wouldn't drink. Of course I was wrong. It just took me many years to realize it.

Today I have a beautiful relationship with my mom. I love her dearly, and it's a joy to be with her. She's a wonderful person, and this turnaround between us is a result of my prayer and willingness to respond. I can say something about her I never thought I could — I even enjoy going shopping with her. My mom has a strange habit when she shops. She decides to take something back before she even buys it.

Four months after I told my mom I loved her, I officiated at a funeral in Phoenix. A young man had come to bury his father. His father had worked in construction and died on the job while in his late forties. We had a morning funeral service at the cemetery; then I returned to my office. Later that afternoon my secretary informed me that there was a young man waiting who wanted to see me. It was the same young man whose father I had buried that morning. As I walked out to meet him, I could see that he was very upset. I looked at him and asked, "Fred, tell me what happened since I saw you this morning?"

"Father," he said, "I would have never believed it. I spent all day with my dad's co-workers and friends. They all told me how much he loved me, how proud he was of me." Then he looked at me with tears streaming down his face and continued, "But, Father, he never told me." Then in a softer voice he repeated, "He never told me."

I thought of the tremendous pain that young man was going to carry for the rest of his life because his father was never able to tell his son how much he loved him. I once told this story at one of our Jesuit retreat houses. A man came up to me. He said, "Let me tell you my story." He told me that his father had lapsed into a coma shortly before his death. The doctor told him that his father was dead for all practical purposes. This man had never told his father what was in his heart. Though his father was in a coma he sat at the bedside and told the dying man how much he loved him. Though they had often disagreed, he told his father that he had meant the world to him, and he would miss him terribly. As he spoke, tears came down his father's cheeks.

If any of us were to die today, would the people we love and care about know how we feel about them? Have we told them? If we haven't, then that's a place where God is calling us to respond. When we pray, whatever regrets we feel, whatever misgivings we perceive are like alarms signaling God's call for us to tend to them now.

There is a great American classic that makes this point. The play, *Our Town*, features two New England families, the Webbs and the Gibbses. The boy falls in love with the girl; they marry and have two children. However, the mother dies at an early age, leaving her husband to raise the children. Toward the end of the play the family is celebrating a daughter's birthday. Up in heaven the wife pleads with God to let her go back and be around her family just one more time. She wants to listen to her children's laughter and see the twinkle in her husband's eye. God warns her that she doesn't know what she's asking for.

Nevertheless, she pleads, and God lets her return. After just a few moments she begs God to take her back because what she sees is too painful for her. The family looks at one another, but they don't see each other. They talk to each other, but they don't listen. They take each other for granted.

I've officiated over many funerals, and I've seen people spend extravagant sums of money on them because they think this will make up for the lack of care and attention they failed to give the deceased while they were alive. All too often we don't realize how meaningful people are to us until they're no longer here. Well, people can do anything they want with me after I die. I just want to be appreciated while I'm living.

For example, I have a tendency to put weight on in the winter and take it off in the summer. Several summers ago I was in the process of trying to lose weight. I was drinking Slim Fast and fast-walking two laps around a four-mile lake in front of our house. On one occasion I came home famished and exhausted from the eight-mile walk. I was lying on the couch when my dad walked in, looked at me and said, "Son, you're sure putting on weight." The comment ripped right through me.

Hesitantly I responded, "Dad, I don't need you to tell me there's something wrong with me. I tell myself that all the time. I know how fat I am. All I have to do is look in the mirror. I need encouragement. I need you to see the best in me."

He said, "Son, I only do it because I love you."

Love me? He said that to me because he loved me? Yes, that was true, because that's the way he had been raised. Let me tell you about your problem and you'll get rid of it.

Unfortunately, I often reacted to such comments by going to the refrigerator and eating a couple of dishes of ice cream. Angry and hurt, I would eat more. The words left unsaid were words of encouragement, the very words I needed to hear.

As another example, for eight years I lived in a parish with seven other Jesuits. When I gave my Sunday sermons, I rarely received a compliment from my fellow Jesuits. I was either too loud or too long. I've since come to realize that people who are raised with silent praise are hungry for approval and as a consequence have trouble complementing others.

This often happens in families. In our constant quest for approval we create competition. I remember that when I preached, parishioners would tell me how wonderful my sermon was. However, if the pastor said nothing, I felt a failure. I spent much of my life looking for my dad's approval. The pastor became my surrogate father, and he was also a man of silent praise.

Well, I've found it's worth the risk to complement another. It's worth breaking old patterns and responding in a new way — looking at another and ourselves and seeing worth.

If we were to die tonight, how would people remember us? Would we be remembered as positive, grateful, affirmative — or as negative and critical? What would be the legacy we would leave with the people we love? It's a difficult question, and we may not know the answer. We could approach the people in our family, our spouse, our children, our friends and ask honestly, "Do I bring out the best or worst in you?" Even those we ask may not be sure of the answer or willing to share it.

I have found that people usually respond the way we expect them to. When I was a vice-principal I had the good fortune of following a tyrant (it's easy to take the place of someone like that). He used to make student offenders copy pages from the telephone book. He played cop, and the kids played robber. I treated the kids with respect, and the vast majority responded in kind.

As adults we do that to one another. We have a set of expectations, and we measure success by how people respond to those expectations. If we want the best for our children, our friends, and the people we love, the best way to encourage them is to see them as unique and precious in the sight of God, each in their own way. We don't need to be reminded of how bad or selfish we are. We do enough of that ourselves. What we do need is to continually remind ourselves and others that each of us is special and loved.

The desire to seek honesty and friendship with those we love and care about can come from the contemplation prayer I have described. Understand what I'm saying here. The contemplation is the prayer, not reciting words by rote we learned in our childhood. You must be open to the subtle messages you receive. If you are receptive and act as God directs, you will receive a wonderful grace in your life.

Today as far as I know I don't have a person in my past or in my present life that I can't talk to or with whom I'm not at peace. It's because of this prayer. It would be a wonderful gift indeed, if on our deathbed, we could honestly say, "I'm at peace with everyone."

FEAR OF RESPONSIBILITY

One of the most interesting passages in the Bible is the story of Creation in Genesis. If you look closely, you will see there are two versions. According to one of them God created each of us in his image, male and female. It is our responsibility as children made in God's image to become whole. We do that by integrating the male and female components of our personalities. I may use examples of husbands and wives here, but this applies to all of us — the single, widowed, divorced — because everyone is on a journey to wholeness. What I say about men applies to most men but can also apply to women and vice versa.

In this vein the challenge for men today is to develop their feminine side. In order to become whole a man must learn to listen to his heart, share his feelings, and express his emotions.

In our society the prevailing tendency is for men to be all male like the motion picture images of John Wayne or Clint Eastwood. However, if a man doesn't experience his emotional, sensitive side, then the older he gets the more moody he becomes as he slowly withdraws from life. Moodiness is the inevitable consequence of burying our feelings.

The lack of emotional development in a man is also indicated by a sad reality. There is a high statistical probability that when the wife dies first, the husband quickly follows; however, if the husband dies first, the wife far more often goes on to have a normal life span.

The inevitable result when a man doesn't develop his own emotional life, his own sensitivity, is that he gradually becomes more dependent upon the woman for his emotional life. As he grows older, he literally can't live without her.

The greatest challenge for many women is to develop their masculine side, that is their assertiveness as a woman. Now, there is a big difference between an assertive woman and an aggressive one. The distinction comes from the source of these behaviors; assertiveness comes from self-esteem while aggressiveness originates with anger.

If a woman is to become assertive, she must develop her own life and make her relationship with herself the most important relationship she has. The greatest gift that a woman can give to her children and husband is herself. A woman who never develops her own personal life, her own individuality, will make her husband or children her world. In time she will become an angry woman — angry at her husband because he didn't save her — or a very talkative woman who repeats all the things she's heard, and since what she hears isn't connected to the person inside, it comes out as chatter. We've all seen it — the moody man married to the talkative woman. That is what happens when wholeness doesn't take place.

We all know there are profound differences, not just physical, between men and women. Many books have been written on this subject. From cradle to grave these gender differences are always with us. Brothers and sisters raised by the same parents seem to come from different worlds, or as one best selling author suggests, from different planets. From an early age boys and girls think, feel, speak, act, and even play differently.

Studies have shown that boys tend to play outside in large groups. Their games are aggressive and physical; they have winners and losers. They have many rules in their games that are debatable. Boys instinctively crave freedom and independence.

Girls on the other hand play games in which they can take turns or play house where there are no winners and losers. They play in small groups or in pairs, usually with best friends. Girls intuitively crave intimacy and cooperation.

My experience has been that too often the lack of understanding between the sexes is replaced with animosity. We've all noticed that men and women have trouble with each other. We all need to know and understand these gender differences in dealing with the complexities of male and female relationships.

I used to belong to a racquetball club, and in the men's locker room I often heard the cliche, "Women. You can't live with them and you can't live without them." A friend once approached me with the comment, "You know why women live longer than men? They don't have wives." Recently I heard the story about a man doing eighty miles an hour down the highway. Suddenly he heard sirens and saw the lights of a police car closing in on him. He sped up to 90, then 100, and finally 120 miles an hour, but still the police car closed on him. Finally, realizing it was useless, he pulled to the side and stopped. The angry officer demanded to know why he had tried to outrun him. "Last year," the driver explained, "my wife ran away with a cop and I thought you were him trying to bring her back." There are scores of jokes with both sexes serving as the brunt that capture this misunderstanding we have between the sexes.

Many men want women to keep the house clean, cook a good meal, and make love, but not to become overly emotional. When a woman is emotional, most men start looking for an exit. It is typical for a man to express the attitude, "I work hard all week. When I come home, I expect it to be peaceful and quiet." It is common to hear from a man, "There you go again. Why do you always have to be so emotional?"

Emotions can be very transitory and unpredictable. We can love and hate the same person during the same half hour. If a man doesn't understand his emotions. How volatile they can be. He will react to them as if they are permanent — with disastrous consequences!

However, men need to understand that they will never come to appreciate the emotions in a woman until they appreciate the emotions they have within themselves. As long as a man gives no importance to his own emotions, he will always give little or no importance to them in a woman. It's the macho male who tells the dirty stories and downgrades women in the locker room. It's the macho male who is so uncomfortable with his own emotions that he devalues women. Until a man understands the importance of his own emotions, he cannot honor their place in the lives of others.

Women experience their own difficulties with men. I've heard many women say, "Men just don't get it." Men often react with inflated egos and become wrapped up in themselves. It is usually the woman who feels she must compromise in a relationship with a man. Men have their own freedom, their own personal lives which are usually centered outside of the home.

It is all too common for a woman to feel a prisoner of the home or of a relationship. She will put her own friendships and activities on hold to adjust to her partner's needs; she may wait all day for his telephone call. But a woman will never come to appreciate a man's need for freedom or a personal life until she develops one with herself. As long as a woman doesn't have a personal life, she will begrudge her own limited existence and not comprehend that need in a man.

In the vast majority of conflicts that exist between husbands and wives, the problems most often center around the emotions of the woman and the man's need for freedom. A vicious cycle ensues as a man desires more freedom and a woman becomes increasingly emotional.

This common conflict is rarely resolved in a marriage as long as each believes the other has the problem. The husband thinks if only his wife had more control over her emotions they would have a better marriage. The problem, however, is not with her display of emotions but with his underdeveloped emotional life and lack of understanding.

The wife, on the other hand, assumes that if her husband wanted to be around her more often and if he would give her half the attention he gives to his friends and his job, she would be happy. The conflict isn't over the amount of time he spends or lack of attention he gives her. The problem is she has made her husband her personal life, the center of her existence, and, consequently, has placed too many obligations on the relationship. Neither partner wants to do what they have to do.

In order to understand this conflict, we have to understand why people fall in love. What is it that brings two people together? Here's the macho man, free and easy as a bird. Suddenly, he's in love and singing in the shower, writing poetry, and experiencing feelings he's never felt before.

From my years of teaching American Literature to high school boys I made an interesting observation. I could not teach literature to a young man until he'd fallen in love. It's this experience which opens up so much about himself, which develops feelings, and emotions he never knew existed. A young woman is also growing and changing — looking for her "prince" to rescue her from the here and now and carry her off to an exotic, exciting, fulfilling future.

All this may seem a bit cliched, but within it is the fundamental notion common to our experience of being "in love." The reason we experience bliss when we're in love is because we feel whole. During the initial phase of love, the man is in touch with his emotions while the woman experiences power. When a man and a woman are in love, they are joined as a couple and together they feel complete.

Being in love is a marvelous gift. Too often, however, infatuation is confused with genuine love. Infatuation generally lasts about eighteen months, just long enough to cause great harm since it is all too common during this time for a couple to marry. Then one morning they wake up and realize they married an ordinary human being. It is when infatuation wears off, when the glow becomes tarnished, that so many marriages begin to disintegrate. Each spouse thinks he or she made a mistake. After the first few months he thinks she's too much like her mother; she thought he would be different. He gets involved in his career, she becomes involved with the children, and they increasingly go in separate ways. I've known couples who were married many years, but once their children left home, the parents had nothing in common. Many of these marriages end in divorce.

There is a legitimate place for infatuation because it's the invitation to love and the motivation to love, but it's precisely when infatuation wears off that real love begins; love is not primarily emotions, and it's certainly not dependency.

Bear in mind that the more whole we become, the less dependent we are. The less dependent we are, the less fear we have. We don't need others to find ourselves; we need others to share ourselves.

It is in the context of our desire to be whole where spirituality and sexuality merge, for the only authentic way to talk about sexuality is in terms of spirituality. It is the only thing that makes sense to me.

Let me bring all of this together. There is always a reason why we're attracted to, fascinated by, or find ourselves dependent on someone. That reason is spiritual. We're attracted to somebody because that person has something we need in order to feel whole. That's why we become drawn to another. It is not the person that arouses our interest but "it" — the something we need, something we lack.

Whether the relationship be romantic or a close friendship, there is always a reason why we're attracted to someone. One of my own characteristics with which I struggle is my compulsion to be responsible to excess. As a consequence, the kind of people to whom I'm attracted are free spirits. It should come as no surprise that that's the area I need to develop in my own life.

Free spirits, on the other hand, are usually attracted to responsible people because they need to develop their sense of responsibility. Intuitively, we understand that the people to whom we are attracted can be our teachers.

I have a tendency to become involved in projects with these free spirits. After a few months I end up doing everything while they do nothing. What exacerbates the situation is that I'm the kind of person who feels guilty about everything, so I get involved with people who don't feel guilty about anything. If I don't develop within myself my own free spirit (and it's another free spirit who can best teach me), and if they don't develop responsibility within themselves (and I can best teach them that), then that which has brought us together will eventually drive us apart. I become angry with them because they do nothing, and they yell at me for trying to control everything.

A man who can't live without a woman is often a macho male who hasn't developed his own emotions. He needs a woman around to be his emotional life. A woman who can't live without a man is often one who doesn't have a personal life, so she needs a man to whom she can attach her identity. We all know stories of women who divorce alcoholics and then turn around and marry another. Until these women learn to rescue themselves, they will continue to get involved with people who need to be rescued.

I've learned one technique from watching the O.J. Simpson murder trial. When somebody says to me that their spouse should do this or that, I say, "Objection overruled," but when they say to me that they themselves should do this or that, I say, "Objection sustained."

Love is work. It requires our attention and needs nurturing. After infatuation fades, we're faced with the challenge of taking responsibility for our own happiness and not placing it on someone else. The journey to wholeness consists of the steps we take in growing and learning from our relationships when we become responsible for ourselves.

As a man, I can speak with more personal knowledge about our reactions. Most men show little emotion, and the emotions they have are often those that revolve around sex and anger. Men have a tendency to suppress their anger since experience has taught them that uncontrolled anger is dangerous and in doing so they also suppress their emotions with it. It is common that suppressed anger in men is manifested in energy to control their wives and families.

A man who fails to develop his emotional life doesn't learn to express what's inside his heart and as a result is only half a person. His children will never experience his sensitive side. If a man is ever to get in touch with his emotions, he has to release that anger. Only when he releases it, can he experience the full spectrum of his emotions and find that he can be sensitive, gentle, and tender.

So why are men so angry?

Rollo May provides an interesting answer. He writes that most fathers use the corporate model to order their family. They plan their children's lives as if they are commodities. These fathers give them things but refuse to share their hearts. They give their children advice, but they never listen to their children in return.

Most men are angry at their fathers because their fathers never shared their hearts with them. Until our recent industrial society, fathers took their sons to the wilderness and taught them to fish and hunt. They showed them how to tend the land, how to survive. Today many sons encounter a father who comes home exhausted from the corporate world, and they spend their time together watching television. Think how many fathers and sons you know who can only discuss sports. It's their single common ground.

We are reluctant in our society to acknowledge the tremendous power exercised by corporations over our lives. I discussed earlier the unhealthy influence it has over Christmas and child rearing. One of the unresolved questions about HMOs is that life and death decisions are made by corporations and not physicians. It can potentially become capitalism run amok.

Whatever the reason, for men anger is the issue. How much of a controller are we? How much do our wives protect us? If we are in a bad mood, do we put everyone else in a bad mood? When a driver cuts in front of us, do we react as if they've been planning to do it for years? Can we talk about politics without becoming agitated? The point is we are already angry, and the incident or topic brings that anger out in us.

Women tend to grow more spiritually than men. The most common problem that is brought to me during missions is when a woman says, "Father, I'm growing spiritually but my husband isn't, and I don't know what's going to happen to our marriage." It's true and a genuine concern.

A woman's greatest fear is the fear of loneliness. She is much more likely to expend her energy on people, and we grow more from people than we do from the marketplace.

A man's greatest fear is the fear of failure, and if he doesn't overcome that fear, he will spend his whole life in the mar- ketplace. All he'll have to show after forty-five years of work are a gold watch — and an ulcer.

I've known men who have gone bankrupt, men who have lost everything they spent their lives striving to acquire. I've come to them and asked if I could help, if I could be their friend, and they respond with, "Oh, I'm fine; I can handle it." I've known very few men who are able to ask for help. We can play golf and do activities together, but it's difficult to share ourselves.

During my dad's last few weeks alive, he lay in his bed with this wonderful smile on his face. He would look at mom and say, "What a beautiful family. There is so much love in our family. We're so lucky." My dad's greatest consolation on his death bed was that he was surrounded by a family of love.

Watching this I thought to myself how lonely it would have been for my dad to be surrounded by a family who didn't know him and one which he didn't know. What a tragic way to die.

One of the greatest experiences I've had as a priest was on the last Sunday my dad was alive. It was my parents' 54th wedding anniversary, and I presided over the mass in which my parents renewed their vows. After mass my dad called each one of his children individually to say "goodbye." He died the next day.

For men the greatest gift they can give their wives and children is not what they provide but the gift of themselves; it's the gift that lasts forever.

The greatest challenge for a woman after infatuation fades away is to develop her own identity, an identity separate from the successes or failings of her husband and family. A woman is an individual with many gifts for this world. It's vital for a woman to discover an identity in which she can invest her time, energy, and creativity — be it a career, special interest, or ministry in the church. A woman who doesn't develop her own individuality is only half a person.

My mom is a classic example of this. She had her first art class when she was sixty and her first exhibit when she was sixty-five. The only art I remember her doing when I was a young boy was drawing Santa Claus for Christmas.

During the final years of my dad's life, my mom waited on his every need and in doing so gave up her own personal life. She stopped painting, meeting her friends. Once he was gone she experienced terrible loneliness since she had no life independent of her husband. She remained essentially house bound, talking to my dad's pictures. Slowly she has improved and is beginning to enjoy life. The more she goes out with her friends, gets back to her painting, the more she develops her personal life, the more she enjoys living. She no longer gives reasons why she can't do something; she finds reasons why she can. The greatest gift a woman gives her husband and her children is not mothering them, not taking care of them; it is the gift of herself. That's the gift that lasts forever.

If we don't develop that other half, problems will inevitably arise in the relationship and will, by necessity, create an ever widening chasm between us and our spouse. It is not the fault of the other. We should focus on developing our own selves.

As a way of bringing all of this together, I would like to give both women and men a final challenge.

Women must ask themselves very honestly: Do you take the man in your life personally? Are you easily hurt, overly sensitive? If that is true, the man in your life may truly love you, but he must always worry about your reactions. You've created a relationship of eggshells. Don't be afraid of the truth. The more you develop a relationship with self, the less personal you will take your husband. That's what your kids mean when they say, "Hey, mom, get a life." The more you have your own life, the less personal you take others and the easier you are to be around.

Recently, three of my married male friends joined me at one of my missions. They played golf, surfed, had a wonderful time. However, the night before they were to return home, they became moody. They were afraid of the reactions of their wives when they returned. One of them said it so well, "If only our wives could go off with their friends and have a wonderful time, then they would know how important it is for us." Too often wives are simply sitting at home waiting for their husbands to return. They feel meaningless until their husbands are with them.

Men must ask themselves honestly if they understand how important thoughtfulness in little things is to women? Most men don't. Men generally aren't thoughtful to each other in small things, and they carry that over to their relationships with women. When Mother's Day comes along, the energy I spend finding the right card with the right sentiments is more important to my mom than how much money I spend on a gift. Recently, I was at a parish where the pastor told me that for many years he had his secretary buy his cards for his mother. Always after a visit with her his mother would say, "Be sure you tell your secretary thank you for all the beautiful cards."

I've seen many men bury their wives. I've seen the coffins surrounded by flowers and wondered how often he sent her flowers while she was alive.

During one March it rained the entire month in northern California. My mom loves her garden, but she couldn't work in it because of the rain. I sent her a European Basket, which is a variety of plants, so she could have a garden in her own home. She reacted as if I had sent her a million dollars. She was so touched that one of her children was thinking about her and knew how much her gardening meant to her.

A few years ago my entire family convened to celebrate Thanksgiving. After eating, everyone gathered in the living room to visit. While they were doing this, I snuck into the kitchen and cleaned everything up. What made my Thanksgiving special was to see the expression on my mom's face when she walked in and saw that clean kitchen. There's nothing that causes me greater happiness than to make the people I love happy.

From my many years of counseling and from everything I've learned, if I were married today my first thought in the morning would be to see what I could do for the woman of my life that I don't have to do. We know how wonderful we feel when someone does something for us that is unexpected or not required. It makes us feel esteemed and cherished.

The greatest challenge in a man's life is not to build a successful career but to develop his heart. He must share his emotions and rid himself of anger so the people who love him, especially his wife, can know his heart, whereby he can be a whole person to her.

The greatest challenge in a woman's life is to realize she's much more than a doer. She's not there simply to nurture and care for everybody, but to share herself as a unique person. The greatest gift she can give her husband is not to take care of him — for that's what mothers do — but to be a friend, a companion, and to share her heart.

I believe one of God's greatest gifts to us is the opportunity to have a soul mate with whom we can spend the rest of our lives. It's a great, visible sign of God's presence in the world. This never happens by accident. It only happens if we work at it. Love carries the responsibility of developing and sharing our wholeness.

Chapter Seven

FAMILY SPIRITUALITY

7

In the first part of this book we discussed personal conversion, allowing the person inside us to accept the good news of Jesus Christ. Then we moved to marriage and the unique dynamics in that relationship. Now I am turning our attention to family spirituality.

Developing family spirituality is essential because our families are the most important realities in our lives. This poses a difficult challenge for us, however, because it is much easier to take risks with strangers than it is with the people who really matter to us. After all, when the chips are down, our family is all we really have. Many people prefer not to take the risk rather than take it and fail.

I described earlier how my family experienced deep love and peace during my father's funeral. It is part of my ministry to share this story of my family's journey toward spirituality in an effort to help others achieve this. Healthy family spirituality does not necessarily equate with strong family religiosity. It's wonderful to express our spirituality in religious ways, but this is not what spirituality is about. We can pray in the first pew of church, recite the rosary, and read scripture together, but that doesn't mean we talk to and trust one another. It simply means we observe the outward signs of worshipping together.

It's my opinion that in the past families tended to be more family centered than they are today. I grew up in a neighborhood where everybody knew each other. The moms took turns preparing lunch for the neighborhood kids. We spent the day playing various games in the street and yards, and spent the evening with our families at home.

Today a fundamental change has occurred in our society. We have become transient with families moving frequently. Often we aren't friendly with our own neighbors. Today we can live next door to someone for years without knowing their name. Parents are afraid to let their children venture outside of their home. To protect them and keep them from getting into trouble we involve our kids in organized activities. Soccer leagues and little league games have, unfortunately, taken an over emphasized role in many families.

Some families have children in two or three schools requiring meetings, commitments and activities that take time away from the family meal. As a result, we've created a generation of self-centered (as opposed to once family-centered) kids.

Those of us who have worked in schools see it in the decline of common courtesy. For example, students don't use trash receptacles in eating areas. They toss everything on the ground and expect someone else to pick it up. Now this may seem insignificant, but it's only one example of a pervasive problem. Young people today often lack awareness and sensitivity.

When I was a prefect of discipline, I took students to sports tournaments, and we stayed in hotels. Many of these students made as much noise at three o'clock in the morning as they did at three o'clock in the afternoon. They didn't want to cause trouble, but they were just not aware that other people were sleeping.

When we center everything on our children, they come to believe the world centers on them, and this attitude doesn't suddenly change with adulthood. When two people marry and each thinks the world centers on them, it's very difficult for the relationship to work. If parents center everything on the daughter, when she marries and has children, she finds it very difficult to be a mother. The hardest job in the world is taking care of an infant twenty-four hours a day. All too soon she can't wait to get back to her job and place the baby in day care.

Too many parents have forgotten the greatest gift they can give their children is their love for one another. When kids are made more important than the marriage, we create self-centered kids. We give children what they want, not what they need. When as young adults these children go into therapy their issues concern not getting what they needed.

In our culture people fall in love and marry before working out these earlier issues. Before they have taken the time to properly examine their life and its future direction, they become caught up in the rat race. Because they haven't dealt with their issues it is easier to put their energy into the kids than into the marriage.

So, how can we become family-centered in the modern world?

For spirituality to become the binding, directive force within a family, the father must become the spiritual director. It is the father who determines the role of spirituality in the family as a family. If the father is present, he assumes that role in most households. While it is the mother who is the core of unconditional love. Her love is the nurturing love, but it is the father who sets the spiritual example. Traditionally, without his guidance spirituality as a family is stunted. The reason is because if the father makes his career more important than the family, the family will become angry because he has misplaced his priorities. That anger interferes with their developing family spirituality.

This is not to say that individuals within the family cannot be spiritual. They can, but for the family to have spirituality, the lead must come from the father. I do not suggest that this is necessarily the best model; it is rather the one our culture has given us.

If we don't make the spiritual our highest priority, then whatever else we've given the greatest importance in our lives will control us. It's next to impossible for us to build a stress-free balance between material and spiritual values. Imagine what it would be like if all life decisions were made easily, and the material and spiritual aspects of our lives flowed in harmony. In our culture it's a ceaseless struggle between the two because there is so much emphasis placed on appearance and possessions. We live in a materially affluent society and that makes the competition especially keen.

There are times when we have to make a decision about what is more important in our lives. For example, where do we choose to spend our free time and with whom or what do we commit ourselves? Those of us who work daily must ask ourselves how willing we are to make the commitment that the most important priority in our lives is not our jobs nor what we have but what is inside of us. It's not what we do but what we nurture and share with others that is our greatest gift.

I have mentioned my dad's decency many times and told you about the love in our family during his final days. My dad, drinking or sober, worked hard at being a good person.

My dad was a success in business, but the more he succeeded the more his company demanded of him. He understood this, and though he often worked long nights and Saturdays, he still made a point to find time for family. On Friday he often picked us up from school and took us to a park for family picnics. There he taught us sports and other lessons of life. Sunday was always family day. We attended mass followed by breakfast prepared by my dad — then mom spent the rest of the day cleaning up.

These were important events in bringing our family together. The reason we became a loving family is because my dad ultimately made the family more important than his job.

Our culture has taught us that men are providers, that their importance in the family lies in what they do and how much they earn. Consequently, many fathers make their careers their highest priority.

In single parent homes the need for and difficulty in developing family spirituality is even more acute. It would take a book in itself to deal with these problems. Single parents are faced with the daunting challenge of balancing their limited time and energy between their careers and their families. The struggle to survive and provide a safe and comfortable home for their children can easily overwhelm all other needs. They face a nearly overwhelming obstacle in creating family spirituality and must place even greater importance on the entire message of this book.

In our society, we fight a constant battle between the values of the material and spiritual. I have always found it interesting how much money is spent on funerals and weddings. In our culture it's very expensive to die or get married. Money is lavished on meals, clothing, and nice locations when the real meaning lies in the ceremony and the exchange of words. Perhaps we should throw a celebration for couples who have been married 25 years instead of when they are just starting.

We struggle every day with this battle between the world of appearances and the world of the heart, and we must be sensitive to how difficult this struggle is. The greatest gift we have to share is the gift of love within us. This gift of love is what Jesus Christ asks us to call, "Father." This gift is most often manifested in doing ordinary things with extraordinary love. Nothing in the family will change unless we commit ourselves to discovering and sharing that gift.

THREE DEVASTATING RULES

If we are ever to deal responsibly with our families, it is essential that we know our individual stories. Each of us has a history, our own story, that is based on the way we were raised, the way we related to our parents, and the patterns of behavior that were set in our childhood. Until we deal with that story honestly, we won't understand the intimate forces that have shaped our lives. Today we struggle with these ghosts of authority from our past, that "committee" in our head. Not only are those voices strong but also the personalities and behaviors of our parents often become unconsciously ingrained into our own patterns of behavior as we age.

We are taught in school that without education of past events, history will repeat itself. The same is true on an individual level. If we don't become conscious of our story, we will continue to repeat it.

My response to individuals who ask me whether they should marry a particular person is to tell them to take a close look at their boyfriend's father or their girlfriend's mother because it's very possible that's what he or she will be like in twenty years. There is a very high percentage of marriages that eventually become just like the parents' marriages.

There seems to be a mechanism, which I call our parents' symbolism, that drives us to live out our childhood as adults. Social scientists have discovered a high statistical average of people who die in the same manner as the parent from whom they sought approval. In their last act it's as though they're seeking final approval from that parent. This parental symbolism is such a strong force that we often don't deal with it until we're in extreme emotional pain and are compelled to.

Let me share my story with you. My parents were fine people who tried to do their best. However, for years I never wanted to take an honest look at my childhood. When people asked what kind of childhood I had, I told them it was wonderful because I had wonderful parents.

When I became older and took on more responsibilities, I realized there wasn't a person to whom I felt close. I was dying of inner loneliness because there was no intimacy in my life. I was in deep pain and didn't know the reason. I couldn't understand why I had difficulty connecting with other people, being there to love, accept, and enjoy the things that others had to offer.

When I looked back at my childhood, I realized it was not as perfect as I pretended to believe. My dad had been a heavy drinker, and I remember at five or six years of age not being able to go to sleep until I heard the garage door open. There were many nights when the garage door never opened, and I would toss and turn the entire night because my father never came home. When he finally did, my mom and dad argued. After which my mom gave him the silent treatment, filling the home with tension for weeks. I remember the terrible pain and loneliness I felt as a child living in a home with parents who didn't speak to each other.

Because my mom couldn't drive, my dad did all the driving for the family. There were many times when he was drunk and would drive with us kids in the car. One time he accidentally drove up a steep, dirt fire road at night. When the car reached the top of the hill, we could see it was a dead end with a sheer cliff that dropped off beside us. There he was backing down this narrow road in the black of night, just a few feet away from the edge of the cliff — and drunk. It was a frightening experience, and there were many others.

At parish picnics, when everyone played horseshoes and volleyball, I kept one eye on my dad to see how much he was drinking because I knew he had to drive us home. Throughout my childhood I was obsessed with my dad's drinking. As a consequence, I didn't develop my own life since I was preoccupied with my parents' relationship with each other. The consequence is that I became a rescuer, and for many years of my life I was focused on others. The innocence of childhood was replaced with worries and anxieties. In order to escape all this I joined the Jesuits when I was seventeen years old — and became a professional rescuer.

Growing up in an alcoholic family was very painful even though my parents were loving people. I know from my own drinking how hard I tried to be good in my life just as my dad had. In fact, I tried harder to be good when I was a drinker than I do today, and I know that was the case for him. There are nice people who are nice drunks, and mean people who are mean drunks.

Throughout my childhood years I never talked to a single person about my dad's drinking. It was as though it didn't exist away from my family. If anybody asked me how I was doing, I always responded by saying I was doing fine. That's how I was during my childhood, always doing fine, no matter how much personal pain I suffered. I didn't pay attention to any of the feelings I pushed deeper and deeper inside me. I buried my anger and pretended it didn't exist.

Not long ago I had an interesting conversation with a former classmate who went to school with me from the second grade through high school. We used to double date and play sports together. Both of his parents, I learned, had died from alcoholism; yet, we had never talked about the problems either of us faced by living with alcoholic parents. Through eleven years of schooling we never mentioned a word of it to one another.

I buried all that pain and, consequently, learned never to communicate and share what was inside. My personality was built by focusing on my parents, their behavior, and their relationship. I did not concentrate on my own needs. I buried my own feelings and was preoccupied with rescuing my dad and blaming my mom for his drinking. I suppressed the anger I experienced towards both of them nearly every day. Since I learned as a child to bury my feelings, I never learned to listen to or honor them. When people asked me how I was feeling I honestly never knew how to answer that question.

Those of us who work with teenagers will likely have experienced this emotional wall. Being a teenager today is a time filled with confusion, inner pain and problems. During my years as a high school vice principal, whenever I asked teens what was going on in their lives, they would look at me as if I were speaking a foreign language.

It's difficult to get teenagers to talk about their feelings because often they have never learned to listen to or deal with them as young children. They reach adolescence, and suddenly we want them to open up and discuss them. They can't communicate their feelings because they've spent all their life burying them.

While I was growing up and hurting inside, my parents weren't there for me because they had so many problems of their own. I learned early in life that I couldn't trust or depend on anybody. I emerged from my childhood with three rules — don't feel, don't communicate, and don't trust.

Suppose as a young man I had fallen in love and married. That young lady would have met and married a man who couldn't feel, couldn't communicate, and couldn't trust. Now wouldn't that have been a wonderful marriage! Imagine how lonely she would have been. It's shocking to think that's how I was prepared to be an adult. There is value to celibacy after all. Just think of the pain I saved some woman by becoming a priest!

When we bury our feelings, our ability to communicate and to trust is hampered. We develop a persona to deal with family problems. Each member in my family developed a different persona to deal with our problems. Being the oldest in the family I became responsible, and that became the core of my personality system.

It's amazing how often children feel responsible for parents. I thought that if I earned A's, made the football team, and worked hard, my dad would stop drinking. I remember threatening my dad six months before I became a Jesuit that if he took another drink, I wouldn't join the order. It didn't work.

I mention none of this lightly. Digging into our past and coming to terms with what happened to us in our childhood is not easy, but it is the key to becoming spiritual.

Those three rules — don't feel, don't communicate, and don't trust — are what many of us have learned, and they cause dysfunction in ourselves as well as in our family. If we are to build a healthy, spiritual family, then we must develop a family life that promotes feeling, communication, and trust.

FEELINGS BEHIND WORDS

You will recall the difference between listening with and listening without an agenda. When we listen without an agenda, we create an environment where our families are safe places to live. In our efforts to encourage the expression of feelings in our family, it is important for us to recognize that feelings tell us what is going on inside us, and they always have something to say.

When people feel things it is most important that we listen to them, that we let them express what's going on inside. All of us feel safe when we can honestly share our emotions. In listening, we should bear in mind that feelings are not thoughts, decisions, or commitments but an important part of what is happening inside us. As listeners it's not our place to tell people how to express an emotion because that teaches others to bury their feelings and that we can't be trusted. When we tell somebody how to feel, we're attempting to mold that person. We're not letting the individual grow from within but trying to form the person from without.

Our feelings are usually different from our words. I learned the importance of listening when I was a vice principal at a high school. Since I was the dean of discipline, teachers sent students to my office with the expectation that I would punish them, but whenever a student entered my office, I first tried to find out what was going on inside him. I never said anything until I heard what feelings or problems the student was wrestling with. Sometimes I had to be very patient and encourage the young man to talk since he was usually afraid of my reaction. He also was worried about being punished.

I often found out what was happening in his life — parents who were going through or had just been divorced, one of the parents had a drinking problem, or the student had been beaten the night before. Yet, it was my job to punish the kid! With the vast majority of students I dealt with, I discovered it wasn't the child with the problem. It was the family.

It was only after I really heard what the student was saying that I knew how to respond. I had to take some severe measures at times but rarely did the kids complain because I honored what they were feeling by listening and that's how I showed I accepted them.

Listening without an agenda means acceptance, and people often erroneously equate acceptance with approval. Too many people accept and approve of others when they're the way they want them to be; when they're not, they express disapproval and punish. That's conditional love. There is not a person I love of whom I can honestly say that I approve of everything they do. I cared about the students who came into my office, and the way I showed that love was by listening. To listen without an agenda, to accept, however, does not mean approval.

Many of us were raised in families where we were taught how, what, and when to feel, and we were punished when our feelings weren't appropriate. Feelings are neither right nor wrong; they simply are, and they're ours. They always say something about what is going on inside us.

We must learn to listen to much more than words. We have to listen to the feelings behind the words because only then will we know how to respond. Since I've learned to listen to my own heart with faith, I've learned to listen to other people without an agenda. If we truly listen to our own heart and believe God is within us, then we can listen to the people we love and know God is with them.

We can't listen to somebody and at the same time be reading the newspaper or watching television. Listening to each other is a sacred act. It's a chief characteristic of unconditional love and one of the greatest gifts we give to another. However, we can't give it to others if we don't first give it to ourselves.

A friend of mine once shared a warm story with me. He moved his family from Chicago to Phoenix, and his nine-year-old daughter had a difficult time adjusting because she had left all of her friends behind and entered a new school. One day she came home and told her dad how much she hated going to school. He stopped what he was doing to listen to her. He asked her a few questions and let her pour out her problems. At the end of the conversation he said, "Honey, when you go to school tomorrow, just make one friend. That's all — just one friend." The following night she couldn't wait for him to come home because she wanted to tell him she had made a new friend.

What a difference he had made in her life because he took the time to listen. If he had been busy or preoccupied, he could have just given her a cliched response, "Oh, don't worry about it. It will get better." However, because he listened openly, God could work.

SHARING STORIES

The second step in building family spirituality is communicating our stories. There should come a time in every relationship between parents and children when parents quit being parents and start becoming friends. How do we make that transition? As I mentioned, it happened in my life with my dad several years ago after I led a retreat for married couples which included my parents.

After telling me of how difficult his life had been, I also learned that my grandmother ran a candy store during Prohibition. She didn't sell much candy because it was primarily a front for selling booze. When my dad was a kid, he was a bootlegger!

One of my grandmothers was Irish, the other English, and they didn't get along for a minute. One would say to the other, "My, you look good — for your age." My dad and mom were both only children who were raised by their mothers. Neither one of them had attended my parents' wedding. How devastating. My dad told me that as an only child one of his greatest struggles in life was that what he did for his wife he also felt he had to do for his mother.

I think there are many men out there who, like my dad, grew to early manhood during the Depression and struggled for everything they had. In the home my dad had to be king. He insisted on having the last word, on exercising total control over everyone in the family. That was how he survived in the work place. That was the father I remembered. That was why we had to get out of the house and go for walks so we could talk openly.

My dad told me things about his childhood I never knew. He told me what his life was like during the years he grew up and how he carried his past into his business relationships. In his ventures he inevitably looked for an older man to be his partner, a man who would be a father figure. Because of the emotional component he brought into the partnership, it never worked out. I could see then how my friendships had been influenced by the emotional baggage from my childhood. He had always been angry with me for rescuing others; yet, he had done the same thing in his business life.

My dad and I fought about everything as I grew up. We couldn't agree on what day of the week it was. There seemed to be nothing we could agree on over the years because we were so much alike.

When my dad told me his story, I recognized that a large part of it was my story too. So much of what he shared with me were events I had experienced in my life. The struggles he had faced were often my struggles. There was never anyone in my dad's life as much like him as me or anyone in my life as much like me as my dad.

My dad used to get mad at me whenever I did the same things he did. These were behaviors which he couldn't accept about himself, and as a result, he would take this anger out on me. If you have a child that you constantly fight with, it is very likely that child is very much like you. When he shared his story, I at last was able to share my own with him. It was a wonderful and bonding experience filled with laughter and some tears. Instead of picking on each other, we shared both the scars and the wisdom gained from what we had each experienced in our lives.

After we shared our stories, my dad and I took trips together, and those were some of the most sacred moments of my life. I'm grateful for these times together because I can honestly say my dad and I were friends when he died.

Like a lot of alcoholics I thought that when I gave up drinking, the rest of my life would fall into place. Sobriety was, in fact, just the beginning. When my dad quit drinking, it was not easy on my mom, and that is not unusual. Like many women married to alcoholic husbands, her life was focused on the recurring cycles of the illness. Once that was gone, the behavior of the alcoholic still remained with my dad but without the drinking. My mom was forced to deal with a new set of problems that dad's drinking had masked for so many years. Because of my own similar experience with sobriety, I was able to understand what my parents had gone through. In time, most of those issues were resolved between them, and what emerged was a better marriage.

We have to know someone before we can love them. That's how we move from being a role, a persona, to being a person. I should have figured this out a long time ago because when I taught high school, I was a successful and popular teacher. My students loved my telling them stories about my adolescence because the kids could see I was human, not some robotic teacher on a pedestal. It's amazing how many parents forget their own adolescence when they have adolescents; the wildest kids become the strictest parents, in my experience.

I told them of the time when my mom, sister, and I were walking along the Russian River, and my mom screamed when we encountered a rattlesnake in the middle of the road. I was only six years old at the time, but I've been deathly afraid of snakes ever since. Shortly after I told my students that story, I took forty of them to the Grand Canyon on a camping trip. The clever little angels found a harmless garter snake and put it in my sleeping bag. I'm surprised my hair didn't turn completely gray!

I enjoyed a wonderful relationship with my students because I shared my life with them, and as a result, I was real to them. We can only love someone who is real, and we become real to others when we tell our story.

Can you tell your story to your children? Can you communicate your experience, your childhood, your heart? That kind of communication allows your children to see that you're not god, but a human being just like them, and that you're in this journey together. It creates a stronger, more meaningful relationship within the family.

I believe the hardest experience for any parent is to bury one of their children. This is especially tragic because if they haven't already they will never become friends with their kids. The best time to enjoy children isn't when they are infants, children, and certainly not when they are teenagers, but when they have become adults.

Many parents seek to conceal their problems from their children. When I worked as a teacher, many of my former students went on to marry and have children. I performed the wedding and baptized the children that followed and later I encountered them at school. I noticed that when these children had problems, they were usually the same ones their parents had at the same age. When the father came to ask me for advice, uncertain of what to do, I said, "Why not tell them your story." They'd answer, "I could never tell them that!"

IN THE DESERT

The third area is trust. A friend is someone I can trust with my weaknesses. I've learned more about God from friends than from anything else in life. Those who are married may want to reflect on their marriages. Would you describe yours as friendship or an eggshell relationship? All of us have families. When weaknesses or problems emerge, do members of our family trust each other? Reflect on it for a moment. How would you characterize your relationships?

Because we're human, we occasionally hurt those we love, usually through thoughtless or selfish acts. We then experience guilt. However, the worst thing anybody can do is to make us feel more guilt in addition to the guilt we already have. When this happens, all too often we unleash on them the anger we have toward ourselves.

The worst thing anybody can do is to punish us because we're not perfect. There is nothing more devastating in a relationship than for two people who love each other to walk through the house and pretend the other doesn't exist. Both are miserable.

When someone has done something wrong and is hurting, that person is vulnerable. When we make him feel more guilty, that only serves to create a wall of distrust. It's during those moments of vulnerability when the child is hurting that we, as parents, have the best opportunity to listen, to communicate, and nurture within our children their ability to trust and be open with their feelings.

When our children have hurt us and feel guilty about it, we're there either to lift them up and help them grow from it or to make them feel worse. It is then that our children decide whether they can trust us or not. Again, friendship occurs when we are able to trust each other with our weaknesses.

It is a spiritual issue when we find that most of our relationships lack trust. It means we don't truly believe in our hearts the good news of Jesus Christ. While I was giving a mission in southern California, an article appeared in the *Los Angeles Times* about Archbishop Sanchez who had embarrassed the church. I became sad as I read the story. The account was written in such a way as to make it look as if some secret police in the Church had picked the archbishop up and delivered him to a monastery in Africa where he would be isolated and shamed the rest of his life. I thought to myself that this man, a sinner like the rest of us, never had a greater need for the love, the forgiveness, and compassion of the community than at that time.

A few months before this I had been in a parish where the young associate had just died from AIDS. There were no phony excuses, and he lived in the parish right to the end. The parishioners loved him all the way to eternity, and his death brought new life to the parish.

I thought of Peter, who committed the sin of disloyalty. When Jesus most needed his friend, Peter denied knowing him, not once but three times. Jesus didn't fill him with shame or guilt. He asked him three times, "Do you love me?" He gave Peter a chance to make amends, then made him the pillar of the Church.

Jesus chooses the weak and makes them strong. In the early Church the two symbols used on the headstone for a Christian were a fish and a rooster. The rooster represented the cock crowing after Peter denied knowing Jesus the third time.

I trust people who have been broken, who have been "in the desert." I call them fellow travelers. It has been my experience that we find God in our brokenness, and this has the power to transform us into compassionate, caring individuals. I don't trust perfectionists because I don't want to be judged or evaluated. I do enough of that myself. I want to be loved. I only trust people who speak about God who are compassionate.

Somebody once asked me what quality best prepares a person to be a priest. I thought about it. The best quality is brokenness, the wounded healer. The worst kind of priests are those who have never been "in the desert" because they have nothing to say from their own experience. They've created a life that is safe, one that isolates them from the human condition.

We're all sinners. When a friend of mine returned from Ireland, he told me that people who are in trouble there don't necessarily go to their parish priests. Instead, they find the priests "with problems." Why? Because they've been through it all. We trust people who are human.

MEASURING SPIRITUALITY

There are two areas in our society that measure what kind of spirituality we have in our families: How we eat our meals and the role television plays in our homes.

Cross-culturally, meals have always contained an element of ritual, a time when the breaking of bread is sacred. The meal has always been much more than simply eating food. It's a time when people come together and share themselves through the events of the day. It's as true for the priests in a rectory as it is for a traditional family.

The way we eat dinner tells us a lot about the kind of spirituality we have in our families. Do we sit together, offer a prayer, and share the day's events with each other? Or do we watch television during the meal, or eat separately because everyone is on the run?

In the years I have been traveling, I've lived with my parents between missions. When I first came home from the road, we would discuss what was happening in politics, sports, the usual things. Then after forty-five minutes we'd run out of conversation, and we'd turn on the television. We even ate on television trays so we didn't have to talk during the meal. When we started developing inner spirituality, we shared our evening meals at the table and I found them much more enjoyable. We were not simply consuming food but sharing and celebrating our lives with each other.

Likewise, I stay in a lot of rectories, and when the priests have an evening meal, when they come together and share their day and ideas, the experience in that parish is much richer and fulfilling. But when I go to parishes where there is no evening meal, where everyone eats on his own, I feel very lonely. No matter how nice the people in the parish are or how beautiful the church, it is lonely when you eat by yourself.

Many families today congregate around the television, that ever-present screen that occupies a heralded space in our living rooms, family rooms, and even bedrooms. How a family relates to television will, like the meal, show how much spirituality there is within the family. Do we turn on the television to watch specific shows, or to fill the room with noise? It is unfortunate that a large number of families spend what precious time they have together sitting in front of the tube. Families that don't know how to talk to each other will turn the television on because they don't want to make the effort to communicate.

I led a retreat one summer for young couples. Most of them had small children and used the television as an unpaid baby sitter. They had conditioned their children to watching television up to six or eight hours a day. Some studies have shown that children watch television up to 32 hours a week. The father works all week and is tired when he comes home. On Sunday he'll sit and watch seven hours of football. This causes many resentments in relationships. The remote control also causes resentments. There's nothing more frustrating than watching television with a "channel surfer." It's a very sad statement when we would rather watch television than share ourselves and play with the people we love.

Regretfully, turning the television off will not necessarily bring communication within the family. If we can't trust and communicate with each other, then turning the television off will simply add boredom and silence. We can't change things from the outside; change must come from the Spirit working within us.

During the 1960s a friend of mine learned his girlfriend was pregnant and they married. When their son, John, was eighteen months old, his mother ran off with another man and left my friend to raise the boy alone. I saw them grow up together, and by the sixth grade the boy was spoiled. He threw a tantrum if he didn't get his way, interrupted conversations routinely; the whole world centered on him. I called him King John because he was the king of the house.

His father realized he had a problem. When he got rid of the television set, it dawned on him that his son had homework and he began helping his son with it at night. They started playing games together in the evenings and were soon communicating. John turned out to be a very likable and responsible young man. To this day my friend will look back and say that the turning point in his son's development came when he threw out the television set.

Now, I'm not recommending that all of us get rid of our television sets. I'm just emphasizing that if we make an effort at developing spirituality in our families, we will discover that television becomes less important in our lives.

What I do recommend is that we have no television on school nights. When we do turn it on, it's to watch a specific program, not to fill a room with noise.

Wonderful byproducts in a spiritual family are enjoyable meals and selective television viewing.

We can sit and nod our heads in agreement with the many important things I've discussed here. We can agree on the need for more sharing, communication, and trust in our families. Yet, we are merely giving lip service if we don't take the time to make spirituality in our family a priority. If we don't commit, then the material world takes over, and it will never satisfy us.

Each one of us knows that. Each of us is looking for God, searching for love. A family centered on spirituality makes this journey together.

✝

Chapter Eight

ANGER

8

The good news of Jesus Christ reveals a God of love, not a god of judgment. There are too many judgmental people in our lives who consider themselves to be religious. Jesus came to show us that through every experience we can come to know and depend on the love of the Father within us. In everything that occurs there is an opportunity for us to grow. It is through this growth that we discover that what makes us precious is not what we have but that we are loved unconditionally. Our purpose in life is to share that love.

It is important that we understand this perspective of Jesus for he viewed things differently than most of us. Our life today is a journey toward discovering that life is about love; it's about sharing that love with family, friends, spouses, and with others we meet along the way. A person grows spiritually in his journey when he first realizes that life is about being, not owning. It's about who we are, not what we do or have.

None of this just happens. In addition to time, it takes a commitment on our part to grow from every experience, whether it be good or bad. It is within this context that life's experiences become opportunities for growth. If we accept this, then anger is a gift, an opportunity to bring us to a fuller awareness of the love we carry within.

People are often prevented from doing this spiritual work in their life because they are paralyzed by anger. They must deal with the anger first. I never became friends with my parents until I figured that out.

Many of us, however, have been taught never to become angry. Anger is viewed as something evil. You should recall that when Jesus threw the money changers out of the temple it was not the first time he had seen them there. He threw them out on this specific occasion because, as so often happens to each of us, he was pushed to a point where he just couldn't cope. He had had it.

All of us have bad days. There's nothing wrong with being angry, but for many of us that "committee" we carry in our heads tells us that anger is wrong and that we're not supposed to act on it. Consequently, we develop negative ways for dealing with the emotion.

ANGERS MANY SHAPES

It is only human to be angry. It is what we do with the anger that is good or bad.

Negative anger may be expressed in several forms. While we may express all of them at times, generally there is a primary means by which we show anger. First, some people vent it in explosive fits of rage. They become mad at situations but don't express it, and it remains bottled up inside them like compressed air. Then some relatively inconsequential event occurs, and they blow their stack.

For example, a father has had a bad day at the office. He comes home and finds a toy or jacket one of his children has left in the living room. When he sees it, he explodes and starts yelling and screaming. After he creates an uproar in the household, he goes into the backyard and works in the garden. He feels good now because he has relieved himself of all that pent up anger. This may be beneficial for him; however, it's upsetting for the people who have to live with him. They never know when these explosive bursts will recur, and they are made to feel responsible for them.

Some people who vent in this manner become rageaholics. They themselves never know what will set them off or what they'll say or do when they become angry. Just as the alcoholic is powerless over alcohol, the rageaholic becomes powerless over his rage. Rageaholics create a family based on anger where, typically, one of the sons himself becomes a rageaholic. In this way it seems to be passed on to the next generation. Though, I intuitively think there are very likely genetic factors at work here as well.

The children who don't become rageaholics often come out of this family system with an attitude of avoidance. They'll do anything to avoid anger and this in itself can be a severe problem. In their effort to dodge anger, they surrender much of their power to their spouses. They never establish proper boundaries because they don't want to experience anger or become angry themselves. Their own anger remains buried and unexpressed.

The second expression of anger is when an individual says, "I'm hurt, I'm not angry." Notice what the person says by using "hurt" instead of "angry." It places the responsibility on the other person; they are being passive-aggressive. These people see themselves as victims. They think when the other person gets their act together, all will be well, but the problem is their own anger, and until they deal with that, they will never feel good about life.

That's the kind I am. These self-made victims have one of the worst problems with anger because they never overtly display it. As a result, they're always hurt.

Since I was taught never to become angry, I never get angry; I get even. I make little comments that "zing" another person. If they get upset, I'll say, "Just kidding . . . can't you take a joke?" I might do things to annoy the other person. If they want me to be on time, I'll arrive a few minutes late. If I was supposed to lock the back door, I'd "accidentally" leave it unlocked. If parishioners thought my homily was running a bit too long and they pointedly gazed at their wristwatches, then shook them as if they were broken, my response was to speak even longer than I had intended.

This kind of behavior is passive-aggressive. If I say I'm angry, I'm the bad guy. When I say I'm hurt, I'm making the other person the bad guy. I shift the blame and make myself the victim. The victim always has to blame someone. We're victims if we feel we would be happy if it weren't for our spouses, children, or parents. We're victims if we typically blame somebody else for our unhappiness.

When I was first a priest, people often took me aside to unload on me their personal tale of woe, to list every complaint and injustice they had suffered. I remained exhausted from the experience. I came to understand that there was a bigger issue at stake here, and I was doing these people no good. I would tell them to go home and tell their problem to the canary, or the wall, because it doesn't matter. When they were ready to do something about it, then I would help.

If what I've described is your form of anger, then you have to own it. It's your issue, not the other person's issue. You cannot wait for the other person to change before you become happy, because that will never happen.

People who allow themselves to be victims over a long period of time, can become permanent victims and utterly powerless over anger. They become obsessed with being a victim and can only talk about the other person's problem.

I've seen this many times in divorces where one partner is so obsessed, so angry at the one they are divorcing that every thought and word is an attack on that person. How does this come about?

If children growing up can depend on their parents' love for each other, they develop self-esteem. But if they grow up fearful of their parents' abandoning them either physically or emotionally, they develop a real fear of abandonment. When these children become adults, they fall in love and marry. They are either going to bring self-esteem or fear of abandonment into their relationships. If they bring this fear of abandonment into their marriages, it becomes the source of the fatal attraction. When they fall out of love, this dependency turns to hatred because their former spouses did not give them the meaning they sought.

By making themselves victims, they become obsessed with getting even. They're powerless over their anger. They'll even turn their children against the other parent. I can't help them because they only talk about the other person, never about their own problems.

Nobody wants to be around victims and they usually lose their friends because people grow tired of hearing them complain and blame. They become increasingly miserable but, of course, console themselves with the certain knowledge that it's not their fault.

The third way people deal with anger is through avoidance. These people never say, "I'm sorry." They never say that they are hurt. They just say they're saddened or deeply disappointed and use this to distance themselves from others. They have many people from their past, even family members, they don't talk to any longer. If they're mad at others, they won't approach them, call them, speak to them, or even acknowledge their existence. Unlike the victim who at least stays connected, these people withdraw. It is a simple way to deal with anger; a person who is a problem simply disappears from their life. Some people have been angry with someone for so long they have forgotten the original cause.

MISDIRECTION OF ANGER

Finally, people can deal with anger by simply burying it and pretending it doesn't exist. They're not victims; they don't hurt; they're not angry — they're nothing. Of all the ways we deal with anger, this method has the most negative impact on our lives and the lives of others because it usually manifests itself in sexual behavior and eating disorders.

When I was in high school, the Church's teaching on sexuality devastated my teenage years. Sex was the one sin that could send us to hell for all eternity, and most of our retreats were based on this single issue. What I was taught about adolescent sex was correct; the way they taught it was harmful. The Church was aware that people were experiencing significant problems with their sexuality but offered solutions that were not helpful.

Without spirituality the teaching of sexuality simply becomes a biology lesson. When children reach adolescence, they begin to experience stress in their lives, and sexuality has two main functions. The spiritual meaning of sexuality is a celebration of intimacy, but the physical aspect is to release tension. This is a bodily function. If a person puts a lot of anger into their body, it produces pressure to release that anger. While masturbation may release tension, it betrays an underlying spiritual issue. It tells us something about what is going on inside us. Instead of calling sex a sin when it is only a symptom, we should deal with anger which is the real cause.

Much of this stress and tension comes from repressed anger. Instead of teaching our kids to bury their feelings (which is what we do when we tell them masturbation is a sin), we need to teach them how to deal with their feelings, their anger, in a positive way. Sex is not a sin; it's a bodily function, and in that context there's no such thing as a sexual problem. Sexuality is a manifestation of what is going on inside and is a reflection of a spiritual problem.

Teenagers are angrier than young children, and this is because they have grown up surrounded by conditional love. As a consequence, peer pressure asserts a great role on their behavior. This repressed anger comes out in sexual activity.

I've met a number of men thirty to thirty-five years old who are nice, have charming personalities, and would make wonderful husbands and fathers. However, they're not married and don't have a family. This sexual energy, which they can't control, is so important to them that when they become involved in a relationship, sexuality takes over, and they never become spiritually connected to the other person. They never develop a bond that can build toward marriage.

I often discover in these men a deep anger toward their fathers. They've buried their anger which is manifested in this sexual energy. The real issue has nothing to do with sexuality; it has everything to do with anger.

For this reason I advise women never to enter into a sexual relationship with a man until he has made a permanent, spiritual commitment to her. She must challenge the man to choose to have a spiritual relationship, one based on friendship, trust, and communication. Sex is like a drug and will otherwise overwhelm the relationship. The problem is that many women come from dysfunctional families and have low self-esteem. They are so dependent on men that they are unable to set boundaries.

Setting aside sexual addiction, which is a disease of itself, there is, in fact, no such thing as a solely sexual problem. Sexual misbehavior is usually a symptom of a more profound spiritual problem. The sexual is reflective of a spiritual problem in which the body needs to release itself from the anger. Forms of masturbation and sexual aggression also stem from this buried anger. The more a person represses anger, the more he must release it. When he begins to deal with anger issues, most aspects of sexuality will then take care of themselves.

The same is true with food; food is not the issue; anger is. Diets may help us take weight off, but the pounds always come back after several months. Diets don't work because they are not the issue. Anger is.

Being passive-aggressive, I don't take my anger out directly on others. Instead, I go straight for the ice cream and take my anger out on myself. That's why I eat. I've consumed a half gallon of ice cream because I've been so angry! I just thank God that it's ice cream and not sex because if I had the same appetite for sex as I do for ice cream, I'd be in a terrible quandary.

Many people try all kinds of diets. They enroll in diet programs, they exercise, and pay enormous sums for exotic health spas without ever understanding that the real issue is not their weight. The issue is how they deal with their anger. If you put bad feelings into your body, you seek out something to soothe it. Food, liquor, and drugs are the most common forms.

Each one of us should take the time to reflect on the way we deal with anger. We need to identify which of the four basic ways we handle it. We need to examine our actions when someone we like or love causes us to be angry. We can't say we don't get angry. We're human, and anger is a part of the spectrum of emotions common to the human experience. The issue is not whether we experience anger but how we deal with it.

TURNING ANGER INTO A POSITIVE

There are practical ways of processing anger in our present lives as well as dealing with anger we've carried with us for years. First, let me address past angers. How do we rid ourselves of the "black books," those annals of anger we've spent years accumulating?

Usually, the thickest black books deal with our parents. More than anyone else in our lives, our parents are the ones we've accumulated unresolved angers toward. It is important for our own spiritual growth that we learn how to forgive them. After all, our parents are among the most important people in our lives. We tend to get angry with those we love the most. The more I love a person, the more I get disappointed, hurt, or angry when that person lets me down.

As children we developed resentments toward our parents because we never knew how to deal with angers and resentments constructively and honestly. Consequently, we buried them inside. Unfortunately, we often carry these resentments into our marriages. A man's relationships with women are filtered through his relationship with his mother. Conversely, a woman's relationships with men are filtered through her relationship with her father. This is so true so often, that at times I have told couples they weren't marrying each other but each other's parents.

The four-step process that I'm about to share with you was designed to help me forgive my parents, so we could become friends. I often approached my dad, hoping we could have that conversation that would open up the gate of friendship between us, but in the midst of our conversation, my dad would push a button. He knew which button to push since he put it there. I'd then leave, angry that I had failed again in my attempt to be friends. When I was angry at my dad, he would react to my anger in kind. When I let go of the anger, my dad suddenly changed. It had always been my issue, never his. This made possible the friendship that was eventually to come.

Even if our parents have died, we still carry this anger into our adult relationships. Let me describe a couple of scenarios that, while stereotypical, illustrate how repressed negative feelings from our childhood can be carried into our adult lives.

A couple falls in love and decides to marry. They have a beautiful wedding and believe they'll live happily ever after. The wife lovingly prepares a splendid dinner every night. She lights the candles and makes it all very romantic when her husband comes home. Several weeks after they're married, the husband is at the office when he suddenly realizes it's seven o'clock. He's normally home by six, but he's been so absorbed in his work that he hasn't called his wife to tell her he will be late. He rushes into his car and quickly drives home. When he enters the house, he's met with an icy silence.

As he tries to say he's sorry, she begins to cry. "Our marriage isn't going to work. It was never meant to be. I know you don't love me."

The husband responds, "I wasn't with another woman. I was just working late!" He wonders where all the anger is coming from.

It is likely that she grew up with a father who worked long hours and spent little time at home. As a child, she always felt second best to his job. Every time her husband overworks, she gets mad at him and experiences all that repressed anger she had toward her father.

Now it's Saturday morning. The kitchen sink is broken, and the husband intends to fix it. "It's our house now, and I've got to learn all this stuff," he says.

The wife thinks differently. "I really prefer you call a plumber," she tells him.

"Oh, no," he replies. "I'm gonna do it."

Later that afternoon the kitchen is a mess and water is everywhere. He calls the plumber and spends four hundred dollars to repair the leaks. The kitchen is finally cleaned up, and they're sitting at the kitchen table. She starts to say to him, "Honey, I told you "

She doesn't get the entire sentence out as his face turns red and he yells, "Keep quiet! Just leave me alone! You don't know what you're talking about!"

She's startled and says, "Hey, no big deal. Don't worry about it. We'll never talk about it again," but she wonders where all this anger comes from.

He probably grew up with a mother who always told him, "I told you so." She may have nagged him all through childhood. Consequently, he built up this storehouse of anger toward his mother. When his wife acts in ways similar to that of his mother, it triggers those angers he's hidden in his black book, and he vents this misplaced anger on his wife.

TOSSING OUT OUR BLACK BOOKS

We must rid ourselves of these black books, the list of angers we carry, if we are to have better control over the emotional forces that govern our lives.

The way we dissolve anger toward our parents is by forgiving them. Even if a parent has died, we still carry them around inside. They're sitting there on our committee, and we remove them through forgiveness.

We give people power over our lives when we harbor anger or resentments toward them. As I mentioned, I would often act like a child when I was around my dad because I held all this childhood anger buried inside. When I released this anger by forgiving him, our relationship improved dramatically.

Some time ago I gave a weekend retreat to men on the subject of forgiving our fathers. Many of these men approached me during the day and said, "Father, I'm doing to my kids exactly what I'm angry at my dad for doing to me." As I've mentioned before, the way we deal with and how we express anger is passed from generation to generation. The only way we let go is to forgive our fathers. If you hate someone, it can transform you and you often become just like them.

There is a very effective spiritual exercise, a four-step process, that has been a powerful spiritual tool in my life. It has alleviated the weight of childhood angers and freed me to accept responsibility. We can use this with anybody with whom we've had problems — a former spouse, one of our children, somebody with whom we have an obsession. However, it's with our parents where we must first put the process to work.

In order to fully participate in this process we need to set aside an entire day and find a safe, peaceful place where we can devote our full attention to what the steps entail. We need a location where we can pray and be with ourselves. I have found that nature helps us get in touch with our souls and recommend a natural setting, such as a lake or a meadow in the woods.

We also have to be prepared to write, an activity many of us struggle with or refuse to do. If I could convince people that writing would help someone they care about, they would write volumes. However, if I told the same people that writing is for their own benefit, I think many of them would feel they're not worth the effort.

Writing is one of the principal ways we can connect with and develop our spirituality, the presence of God within us, and we are worth the effort. Some of us may feel we've already dealt with these issues. However, we may have dealt with them in our heads but not with our hearts. Writing is a way we move from our heads to our hearts. We literally take what's inside us and put it outside in a tangible way.

The first step is to focus on each of our parents individually and recall the five or six most painful events we experienced with them when we were children. We write these down along with our feelings during these events. This will help us immediately get in touch with the feelings themselves.

All of us have "buttons," situations in our lives we react to inappropriately. We overreact because these buttons trigger emotions we've buried from childhood. These feelings we stuffed as children erupt to the surface during specific events in our adult lives. Recalling these situations in our present lives can help us trace the feelings we experienced as children.

We also are conditioned to marry our need, and so we tend to marry the person who pushes our buttons. We should consider what buttons our spouse pushes successfully in order to gain insight into our upbringing. We are not born with buttons; they are given to us in childhood.

Many years ago a priest friend told me a story that he said was one of his most painful moments. He played linebacker on the varsity football team. His father had played college football, and many of the old-timers went to the high school games. During one game the opposing fullback, a huge player, ran over my friend three straight times. The coach called him out, hit him on the shoulder pads and helmet, and berated him in front of the whole stadium. He was so embarrassed that he didn't want to go to school the following week because he thought everybody would be talking about it.

When he returned home from that football game, he was feeling low and vulnerable. His father stung him with a painful lecture and left him with the impression that he had embarrassed his father in front of his friends. His words really hurt my friend who just wanted to hear, "Son, I know you tried." That event affected him profoundly.

As a priest he worked with teenagers both as a teacher and football coach, and he never ridiculed or criticized a student in front of his peers. He never wanted to do to a kid what was done to him. A young man approached him one day and said he needed to talk. "Father," he said. "I'm gay and I have AIDS. I'm dying and I have to tell my parents. I want you there to be with me when I tell them."

The young priest agreed, telling him it was the least he could do. He went with the young man and sat by his side as he told his parents the reality. Their reaction was deeply unsettling. "How could you do that to us?" they responded. Then, "Where did we go wrong?" With a sudden wave of pain this brought back all the negative feelings that the young priest felt about the way he was berated by his father.

I have buttons of my own. For example, I become upset when a person I'm talking to looks at his watch, yawns, or glances around to see who else he wants to talk to in the room. My reaction to this kind of situation goes back to my childhood. I remember as a child sitting in the front seat of our car next to my dad, talking away, when I realized he was preoccupied and wasn't listening to a word I said. I remember thinking he doesn't care; he loves his business more than he loves me. Today when somebody doesn't pay attention to me while I'm talking, it rekindles this childhood anger, and my instinct is to take my anger out on that person.

If I know someone I care about is drinking and stays out late, I become agitated. Maybe he's just enjoying a couple of beers, but, when he returns home, I become angry. The situation brings back all those feelings I had as a child when I used to wait for my dad to come home from the bar.

There are more. A few years ago I was a nice, trim one hundred eighty pounds and felt great. I had been on a regimen and lost sixty-four pounds. Furthermore, it had been four months and I hadn't put a pound back on. I was really maintaining my weight and was quite proud of myself.

In the same way my young priest friend accompanied the man with AIDS, I've had young women ask me to be with them when they told their parents they were pregnant. At a time when they need so much understanding, healing and love, they are met with that same, all-too-familiar, response, "How could you do that to us?" It infuriates me because this was an all-too-familiar refrain from my own childhood.

In one case I was so upset by the reaction of a young woman's parents it pushed buttons of my own. I went on an eating binge and soon gained fifty-five pounds. That's how strongly I reacted to that button.

On another occasion an older priest let me use his car but was obviously uncomfortable with the arrangement. He stood in the driveway with his arms crossed watching me back out, just waiting for a scratch. I was so nervous it took me a half hour! Later the priest joked on how incompetently

I backed the car out. Immediately I was in touch with how my dad used to do the same thing to me.

All of us have these events in our lives. If we give ourselves time to reflect in a peaceful and quiet setting, these events will come to us. We'll know when we get in touch with them because we'll feel them, and getting in touch with our feelings is key here.

Once we've reestablished contact with these painful feelings, we need to communicate them. The second step is to write that person a letter, a letter we will never mail, in which we express everything we want to say. It's important that we touch "on the buttons" because you want to get to the heart of the matter. One of the helps of writing this as a letter is that it allows us to separate the person from the feeling. We'll know if we are truly in touch with these past events because in the second step we'll be writing and sharing our feelings, rather than writing about our feelings. There's a difference. One comes from the heart while the other comes from the head.

There will be raw feelings on the page. We shouldn't concern ourselves with punctuation, spelling, or swear words — just get the anger out and direct it at the person who hurt you. However, no matter how much we vent, we can't end the letter there. We must end with something positive, not necessarily about the other person, but about our life. It's crucial we end on a positive note because as we rid ourselves of the anger, love will take its place. God is within. Once we bring this anger to God, God will heal us.

I was giving a retreat several years ago when a young man asked me, "Father, when did you start experiencing God as love in your life?" At the time I didn't have an answer for him and had to think about it. I realize now that I began to experience God as love when I started to work on my anger many years ago, when I began letting it go. That was when love replaced it.

We may resist delving into the past and digging up all these old events. I'm not telling you that it won't be painful. However, as long as we have anger inside, it will remain with us wherever we go. If we don't begin to resolve these issues now, it is certain we'll dwell on them at some time before we die. The earlier we resolve them, the earlier we'll truly enjoy the gift of life.

RELEASING ANGER

In the first two steps we've not only separated the persons who injured us from the hurt, but we've also created boundaries. Usually, when people have been hurt by others they become enmeshed in resentment and anger. Enmeshment occurs when we fail to separate our feelings of hurt from our anger at the person. By separating the individual from our feelings, we are able to look at that person objectively.

Think of someone who has held you hostage, someone who has forced you to answer to them rather than yourself. When you are involved with that person you are so concerned about keeping the peace that you never realize how angry that person makes you. The first step of this process separates the person from the anger.

In the third step we look at the list of the events from the first step, and then we write down the times when we have done the same thing. Once I recognized that I did the very same thing to the people I love, I realized my dad didn't mean to hurt me. He would have done it to any son he had. The revelation was like a sudden anchor being lifted from my gut. There was a tremendous inner release, and since that moment I no longer take people personally. I used to be easily hurt, overly sensitive, but all that left when I quit taking my parents personally.

I have almost the exact personality my dad had. I've done the same things to people I love that my dad did to me. I've been preoccupied when I've talked to people. I know I've hurt people I care about. I didn't mean to hurt anyone — and my dad didn't mean to hurt me. I know from my own behavior patterns that as I waited for my dad to come home, he wasn't sitting there drinking in the bar just to upset me. It had nothing to do with me. I've done similar things, and they had nothing to do with those who were waiting for me.

I related a story in which my mom told me how angry I used to be with her. Well, I had the same experience with my dad. It was eerie when he said to me, "Son, you used to be so angry with me." The same words my mom had uttered. Now I had always thought with both of them it was the other way around, that they were constantly angry with me.

My mom is a wonderful person, but she married a man who often did not come home until three or four o'clock in the morning. Imagine how she must have felt over breakfast with four children to raise and a husband who didn't come home until a few hours before dawn.

Since my childhood I've never been able to eat french toast or peanut butter and jelly sandwiches because every morning as a child I had french toast and every lunch I ate peanut butter and jelly sandwiches. They were signs of my mom's preoccupation with my dad. She didn't have the energy to prepare something better. My mom did wonderful things for us; however, she was never there for us emotionally when we were growing up. She was never able to share her heart and feelings because she was exhausted from just dealing with my dad.

I've been through similar experiences. I have rescued people who were troubled, and that has created within me the very same dynamics that it did in my mom. I ended up taking care of somebody and completely forgot about everything and everybody else in my life. I didn't mean to do that, and she didn't mean to do that to me.

This third step is very important because we can't forgive anyone until we can let go of taking everything personally. They didn't do it to me; it was their life.

One time I had difficulty talking with a woman whose husband was an alcoholic, and she was unable to accept that he had a disease he was powerless over. "I don't believe that," she told me repeatedly. I noticed she was smoking and asked her if she tried to quit.

"Oh, Father, once I quit for five years and I went back. I've tried a hundred different times to quit smoking."

"You're powerless over quitting, aren't you?" I asked. "If you understand your own struggle with smoking, then understand your husband's struggle with drinking. He's not drinking because he's mad at you. It has nothing to do with you."

The final step is to find someone we trust and can share the first three steps with. We have to own it before we can give it to God and let go. When we tell our story to one other person, we make it real for ourselves.

This four-step process can create a new level of intimacy in our relationships and marriages. Each partner can do the first three steps in his own time and in his own way. Then both partners can come together and share the fourth step with each other. They'll discover that many things they've been doing to each other over the years have actually nothing to do with one another. They'll understand their long list of angers has nothing to do with the relationship but has everything to do with where their spouse came from.

In my work with couples I've found it is essential that they let go of what they have kept in their black books for years. It is one of the most effective tools I have used in marriage counseling as well as with couples planning to marry.

In the field of medicine, doctors are challenged in their treatment of people who have mental illnesses, but instead of taking the time and effort to deal with the problems, because they are overwhelmed, many of these doctors make the easy diagnosis and prescribe a tranquilizer. Many marriage counselors also decide not to work with a troubled couple because there are so many problems that they actually advise them to divorce.

As in the case of medicine, relationships can deteriorate to the point where partners don't want to fix their marriages. Their black books are too thick, and they don't want to put the effort into healing the relationship. It's so much easier to say, "OK, let's get a divorce."

I've experienced some success in marriage counseling as long as both people are willing to enter honestly into the process and give their hearts to it — if not for the sake of the couple, then for the children — the relationship may be healed and strengthened. With God as a centerpiece, we can experience dramatic turnarounds in our relationships with those we love. If we put our hearts into this process, we can reach new levels of trust, communication, and sharing with each other.

Chapter Nine

LETTING GO OF ANGER

9

Many years ago a young priest brought me this story. He was working in a large parish where two of the priests had drinking problems. In fact, they had been sent to a treatment center for rehabilitation; however, the treatment didn't do much for their spiritual lives. What they learned was how to sneak their booze. Back in the parish one of them watched soap operas all day while the other did crossword puzzles.

Still, all of them had duty days. If someone called the rectory and requested a baptism or wedding on a Monday or Tuesday, one of these two priests was supposed to perform the ceremony. My young priest's duty day was Wednesday.

One morning he was passing by the rectory office when he overheard one of these two Fathers say on the telephone, "I'm sorry, we don't schedule weddings on Tuesday. We do that on Wednesday. Could you call back tomorrow?"

My friend felt a sharp ache in his gut. However, he smiled and thought at least he had his heart in his calling and would do a better job. He would witness a hundred weddings while they would have four or five. This went on for several years. He would be exhausted from working this disproportionate work schedule. When one of the drinking priests would ask him a question relating to his crossword puzzle, he would ignore his anger and resentment; then about every six months he'd explode.

One rainy Monday night, on his day off, he was lying in bed exhausted. He had just completed five weddings and six individual baptisms that weekend and was completely drained. He really needed his rest. That evening one of the women in the parish was involved in a car accident. Her family called the rectory that night when it was a duty day for one of these two priests. Her family said she had asked for the young priest.

This priest who took the call walked into my friend's room and said, "A parishioner has been injured and wants to see you."

After determining her condition was serious, but not life threatening, my friend said the duty priest could see her at once, and he would visit her in the morning, but the priest said she insisted on being seen at once. My friend replied, "Father, I'm exhausted tonight. Like I said, I'll see her first thing in the morning, but tonight I need to take care of me. You're on duty. Go and visit her tonight."

"But she wants to see you now," the priest persisted.

The young priest said, "I understand, Father, but I'm just too tired. I can't handle it tonight. I'm too burned out."

The other priest paused for a moment, then looked at the young priest and said, "You're not a very good priest."

Well, that was the wrong thing to say, especially after all the years he had watched this man squander his days working crossword puzzles and drinking himself to sleep every night. He let him have it. Never in his life had he been meaner to another human being. He unleashed everything he had thought and felt about this man for years.

The young priest was so distraught the next morning he was still shaking as if he was having an emotional hangover. That was when he realized how unhealthy he felt and that he needed to deal with his emotions instead of repressing them.

I suggested that he start keeping a yellow pad of paper on his desk and another pad by his bed as I did. Every time I become angry with someone, I write that person a letter because it is when I am angry that I know what I really feel. That is where I put all my feelings, holding nothing back. I use swear words and tell them just what I think. However, I never end the letter until I write something positive. I call this "prayer." Instead of stuffing my anger, I bring it to God, to the love inside me. Every month I burn the letters because I don't want to die in the middle of the night and have someone find them.

If I'm angry at someone, I am unable to sleep because if I haven't dealt with anger during the day, it comes back to haunt me at night. I used to wake up angry and could not go back to sleep. When I began to write these letters, they turned out to be the best sleeping pill I ever took.

This process has helped me overcome many years of buried resentments. Now I get angry at things or events, not at the whole back history. The fact that today I can let myself be angry and grow from that anger has made love work in my life. However, if we're not used to dealing with anger positively, if we've never engaged in any of the activities suggested in these four steps, then we must develop the discipline. Writing is an effective tool because it goes straight to the source of our feelings.

One technique we should use when we're trying to talk to the person we're angry with is to center the focus on our feelings rather than on the other person's behavior. No matter how wrong that person may be, if we attack their behavior, they will become defensive. All we can do is talk about how we felt during the incident.

For example, if you give me the silent treatment and I say you're selfish and manipulative, you will likely respond that I deserve it along with a few other mean things. However, if I say the silent treatment makes me feel lonely, isolated, and unloved, you will be more likely to listen to me. Always share feelings rather than attack behavior.

I was very angry during the period I worked through this material. At the time, I was working on a project with two co-workers. These men had their families, work, and other things going on in addition to helping me. Now, I'm a controller by nature. There's a right way, a wrong way, and there's my way. Whenever I assign work to somebody, that person usually doesn't do it quite the way I want it to be done. This reinforces my belief that I have to do everything myself. Over the period of time we worked together, I ended up doing most of the work while they did less and less. We were fighting, and I was exhausted. The problem was that we were never able to settle this conflict.

However, anger is about my changing, not blaming people. I've learned to stop blaming others because it doesn't work. No matter how much I blame, the dance never changes. With my co-workers, I realized I didn't have to do all the work, and I decided to change myself. If they didn't carry their share of the workload, then the project would not get off the ground.

"I" AND "WE"

There is usually somebody in our lives with whom we periodically become angry. It may be a sister, brother, parent, spouse, or friend. We go through this anger dance in which we get mad, everything settles down for awhile, then we become angry again. The relationship never seems to improve, and the anger dance continues to cycle its way through time. This is a common experience for many of us.

I've learned in life that we can't change anybody; we can't make someone else happy. I've learned that no matter how many times I tell someone or show someone a better way to deal with an issue, I don't have the power to change them or make them do it my way. It's taken me many years to discover this.

In all our relationships there is an "I" and a "We." Whenever a problem comes into the relationship between the "I" and the "We," anger emerges. When there is too much control (when there is too much "I"), or when there is too much dependency (when there is too much "We"), we become angry. Anger lets us know when there is too much control or too much dependency.

Like the red light that flashes on when the engine of our car overheats, anger is a red light that signals something is wrong in our relationship. If the red light in our car didn't go on, we would burn up the engine. So it is in our lives with anger. Anger clicks in to let us know how we can build and improve our relationships. Every time we get angry, it's a call for us, not the other, to change.

A friend and her son used to routinely get angry with each other, and the argument always revolved around the same issue. She had a baby at a time when her marriage wasn't very stable, so her child became her whole world. As a result, she created a spoiled brat who "owned the house." She did all of his feeling for him. When he struck out in baseball, she struck out. When the kids in his class didn't like him, they didn't like her.

Because he was the center of her life, there were no boundaries, and he never learned to face the consequences of his behavior. As he became older, he came to resent his mother's intrusive involvement in his life. He would yell at her to get out of his life, and she would become angry because he ran the house. One day she called me very upset because her son decided he didn't want to go to church anymore.

I told my friend that she should stop fighting with her ten-year-old, that anger is about changing, not blaming. I suggested she quit living his life, give him space to work through his problems, but establish consequences for his actions. She couldn't take him personally because that is blaming, that makes her the issue, and the boy never faces the consequences. If he didn't want to go to church with his family, then he couldn't play with his friends that day. She followed my advice. He tested her once and discovered she meant it. He's been going to church with the family ever since.

She came to realize that kids often strike out and that the world isn't going to end if everyone doesn't like him. Instead of living his feelings for him, she helped her son discover boundaries. Now he's learning that his actions have consequences.

One final example of replacing blame with change centers on the challenges men and women face in becoming whole. I mentioned earlier that a man's greatest challenge is to develop his feminine side, learn to listen to his heart, share his feelings, express his emotions, be tender and be able to let himself cry. The greatest challenge for a woman is to develop her masculine side, her own identity, her own friends, her own interests and hobbies, her own personal life.

You might be interested to know that this same anger dance that occurs between husbands and wives also transpires between priests and nuns. Men get angry at women because they're too emotional, and women become angry at men because they want too much freedom. However, in the secular world that is also what attracts them to one another in the first place.

As I've mentioned, men enjoy being around women because they experience their emotions, a sense of spontaneity and nurturing. Women seek to be with men because they experience the freedom to try something new, something better. They feel the sense of being rescued from the mundane.

Yet, the most frequent conflict that emerges in marriages centers on this point exactly — the man's freedom and the woman's emotions. Instead of blaming each other, each needs to change. He needs to develop his emotional side, and the more he integrates that into his personality, the more he'll appreciate the emotional side of a woman. She needs to develop her identity so she is not looking for a rescuer.

A man who never develops his emotional life is only half a man, and that's all he gives to his wife. A woman who never develops a personal identity is only half a woman. Likewise, her husband can only love her in part.

As with our past angers, there is another four-step process we can follow when we become angry with someone today. If we're committed to changing ourselves rather than blaming others, this process will improve relationships and aid our spiritual growth so that we don't continue stumbling over the same emotional potholes.

The first thing we must do when we become angry is to identify the issue. This is when we may need to go for a walk or spend time alone in prayer and reflection, a time to listen without an agenda. When we become angry at someone, what is it we're really angry at? How does our anger relate to qualities we're attracted to in that person, qualities that we perhaps are lacking?

When a relationship is struggling, there's either too much control or too much dependency — " I " or " We," that's what we must change. You must decide if it's too much " I " or too much " We."

After we determine the issue, the second step is to communicate it to the person with whom we're angry. I had to tell my co-workers I intended to reduce my workload, and that if the business relationship was to continue, they had to do more. One of them now is in charge of my scheduling. My friend had to tell her son she decided not to live his life anymore and that he would be given more freedom, but along with this, there would be consequences for his actions.

A husband might say to his wife, "I know I've been working a lot, and I know I've put too much time into my career. I know I tend to stuff my emotions, and I've taken a lot of anger out on you and the kids. I know I've done that, and I'm really sorry; but I want you to know I'm really going to work at developing my emotional life, and when I need your help, I'll ask for it. I want you to know I'm going to make this a real priority in my life, to try to listen to my heart and share my emotions."

The wife should be just as clear in communicating with her husband. "Yes, I know you have a lot of things going on in your life. You have friends, different interests, and your own personal life. I know I've made you and the kids the center of my life. I know that's the way it's been. Now I want to work on developing my identity. I want to take time to develop my interests and enjoy friends, and I want you to know that."

When we communicate the issues we each must deal with, the other person is given the opportunity to understand and to be supportive.

FACING ANGER

The third step in dealing with anger is to make sure we know which of these negative patterns we use in dealing with anger. We need to know that when we're expressing anger in this way, we only make things worse.

If I recognize that my associate has an explosive temper, then when he rages, I can step back and let him pour it all out. I don't say a word, and I don't need to defend myself. Assuming that he knows he is a rager and that this is a problem for him, then when he's finished raging, I can say to him, perhaps not at that moment, but soon after, "OK, now how can we learn and grow from what just happened?" We move on. If I were to say a word during the rage, I'd make the situation worse.

Conversely, perhaps we'll be working in the office, and I'll make a little comment that "zings" him. He'll say to me, "You're angry, aren't you?"

"No, I'm not!" I'll shout. I've never said "yes" the first time. However, I know when I'm passive-aggressive, it's because I'm angry. I'll reflect for a moment. Then I'll come back and say, "Yeah, there's something we have to talk about."

When I start overeating, that is a sign that I'm angry about something. Recently, I went off my diet and started to eat too much. After a few days I realized that I was angry because I was overproducing again, and my associates weren't around to help with the work.

It's important that I'm aware of my pattern so that I don't stay caught up in destructive behavior. I'd rather discover after three pounds than thirty pounds that I'm angry. When it comes to dealing with anger, whether we're passive-aggressive, explosive, or any other type, we need to be honest about our negative patterns.

The fourth and last step is to be aware of the countermoves. Often in relationships it's a battle over who is in control. Who is right? Who is top dog? We must not let this deter us from our journey. If we give in to it, we'll be right back in the anger dance.

When the wife states that she wants to develop her identity, the husband might counter with, "I'm with you all the way. I want you to do whatever you need to do. I'm one hundred percent behind you. Just make sure you're there for me when I need you. Be certain that dinner is on the table every night at six o'clock."

If the husband doesn't learn to nurture himself, he will always pull that string. If he doesn't learn to take care of himself, he will need his wife to do it for him, and he will deny her the freedom she requires to honor her needs. She has to be aware of his countermove and not let it throw her off course.

When the man expresses his intent to stop burying his feelings, the woman might counter with, "I'm glad you're going to start developing your emotional life. Now let me tell you how." In this case the countermove is one of control (It's all right for you to go out and do what you want. Just make sure I control you.) We have to be ready for responses that may defeat the very thing we desire to change.

ANGER AS A GIFT

Another suggestion I recommend is to never strike while the iron is hot. We only make situations worse when we try to deal with our anger toward someone while we are angry.

We have to allow ourselves space and time to cool down, to work everything out through honest reflection and prayer. We should never pressure ourselves into dealing with anger at the moment. As parents we can teach our children how to use anger in a positive way so that it becomes a gift rather than a destructive force in their lives. Anger can bring us to God, rather than driving us apart.

Imagine a reservoir inside us. Inside this reservoir is all this terrible crud that we need to clean out. The more contaminated waste we remove, the freer we feel. Anger is like sludge that builds up within us and it restricts the natural flow of our feelings. The more we release anger, the less anger we have. Eventually we can honestly say the sludge is gone, that there isn't a single person, place, or institution that we resent.

The word "resent" means angers that are re-sent. If we don't process them, they are re-sent. When the sludge is gone we have empty space to be filled. If we fill it with love and understanding, then there's no room for the anger.

Chapter Ten

THE MEDIEVAL VERSUS THE MODERN

10

Now I want to link what we've learned about the individual and apply it to religion. Since I'm a Catholic, I'll talk about it from that perspective. Today the Church is in a crisis: Is it going to become a museum or a faith community? In Europe following the *Second World War* the Church failed to adapt and didn't address the pain people were suffering. As a consequence, when we visit churches in western Europe, we often go to museums. Today, here, there is also pain, people are hungry, and if the Church doesn't preach the Gospel to the brokenness of our people, our churches will also become museums.

I have never been able to preach what I don't believe. What I'm sharing with you is how I resolved what I learned for myself. I am open to the possibility that I could be wrong. It is important that you understand what I am really saying before you act on it and are certain that you have listened without an agenda. My effort until now has been to discuss spirituality; now I want to connect spirituality to religion, join the two as it were. I am not a theologian so grant me a little slack on some issues.

The Church is in a transition from the medieval to the modern model, and the process is not yet complete. This is the first time in the history of man that a paradigm shift like this has occurred within the lifetime of a single generation. Catholics of my generation were raised in a different Church from the one we find ourselves in today. Just as we've brought our spirituality up to date from the medieval to the modern, we must bring the model of how we look at religion up to date as well.

Yet as I mentioned before, I was taught a model formulated in medieval times, a model that has persisted through many generations. The model emerging today is very different, and we must place our spirituality within its context.

THE CHURCH OF FUNDAMENTALISM

There are four basic differences in how we look at the world today compared to medieval times. The first is in scripture. When I was a young boy, the Catholic church's interpretation of scripture was basically fundamentalism. Three of the subjects we studied in parochial grammar school were U.S. history, World history, and Bible history. Our Bible history books had pictures of Adam and Eve, Noah and his

Ark, and these characters were treated as historical. I can remember arguing with my grandfather when I was in the sixth grade because he believed in evolution and disdained the teaching of the creation. "No, grandpa! Adam and Eve really existed," I insisted. "We can all be traced back to Adam and Eve. Sister told me that!" We were fundamentalists back then, and the Bible was our history book.

In 1943 the Church began the difficult process of change. That was the year Pius XII drafted his encyclical, *Divino Afflante Spiritu*, in which he encouraged Catholics to study the scriptures. This will ultimately have a profound impact on Catholics, far greater than is appreciated today. Before this encyclical the study of scripture was primarily pursued by the Protestants. Most of us old-time Catholics didn't study scripture; we studied Bible history.

Consider how much scientific knowledge has been gathered in the last fifty years. The same explosion has also taken place in scholarship, archeology, religious studies, language, and in our understanding of the development of literary forms. All of this knowledge is available today to study the words of Jesus. For centuries prior to that there had been no new scholarship. It's almost as if we learned for the first time that God's love is unconditional. It is as if this were a new discovery.

In my Irish-Catholic neighborhood in San Francisco, I was raised to believe I had to earn and deserve God's love. Some of us older Catholics may remember the nine First Fridays and how they had to be consecutive. I had a hard time with the consecutive part of it. I went during the school year because everybody did. My problem was going during vacation. It took me a long time to get nine consecutive First Fridays. It meant that no matter how bad I became, somehow I'd meet a priest before the final judgment — I didn't realize it was going to be me.

When I committed a mortal sin, I ran to confession to earn God's forgiveness. If I had died before that, I'd have gone to hell. When I needed God the most, God was in the confessional. I'll ask parents if their kids were in a desperate situation, wouldn't they want to be there for them? That wasn't what I was taught about God. I was taught to earn a "basket of grace" by saying the rosary, attending novenas, with visits to the blessed sacrament, and giving to pagan babies. All these acts were to enable me to earn my rightful place in heaven when I died. While this may be a wonderful way to live, it is not the good news of Jesus Christ.

It's called good news because we don't have to earn or deserve God's love. We just have to accept it with our hearts. However, many of us have that member on the "committee" who keeps telling us we have to be perfect before God can love us, that we have to earn God's love. We cannot hold onto this notion and still be a Christian. That is not what the scriptures tell us.

Some of us have medieval notions of why Jesus died — to open up the gates of heaven, to buy us back from the devil, etc. Jesus died because of what he preached and the way he lived. The Jewish religious institution of his time had created a system where followers could earn and deserve God's love by obeying the institution's laws and leaders, by giving them money, and going to their temples.

Jesus preached that God's love is unconditional, that this love doesn't have to be earned or deserved, that God wasn't found only in a temple. The religious leaders decided to get rid of him because Jesus was leading people away from them, taking away their power. He was a threat to them and that's why he was crucified.

POMP AND CIRCUMSTANCE

After a mere 2,000 years Christianity is just emerging from adolescence. Christianity in America today is based much more on capitalism than it is on the word of God. During these years of adolescence our religion has been more man-centered than God-centered, and we've created God in our image. We've experienced the *Holy Roman Empire*, the *Cru-*

sades and constructed immense, grandiose churches in which to worship. It's been more centered on what we wanted rather than on what God wants.

I believe scripture is an important gift to us as Christians because it will lead us back to the roots of what Jesus is calling us to do. This is a special time in history as we let God create us in God's image. The call of Jesus is more than a particular denomination, doctrine, or dogma, authority or sacrament. It is a whole way of life. It's everything we are.

It was ironic that on the day the *Archbishop of Los Angeles* was being named a Cardinal, I was giving a mission in Downey, California, and the Gospel of that mass centered on an interesting conversation found in the New Testament. John and James approached Jesus and asked if they could be number one and two in his kingdom.

Jesus responded by saying he couldn't promise this. What he could promise was that if they were to be like him, they would have to go through the cross. He further told them if they were ever to be number one and two, they should become servants and not be like the Scribes who missed the spirit of the law. If I were a Bishop, that gospel would constantly call me to conversion. It doesn't matter to me if a Bishop is a liberal or a conservative; what matters is that he be a kind, compassionate, and pastoral man.

The question is whether the institution of the Church or the Bishops have been more affected by history and the divine right of kings than by the message of the Gospel, but I don't want to pick on Bishops. We are all called to conversion. As Christians we must examine our attitude toward the homeless, the poor, those in prison. We can now examine the Gospel and learn God's call for ourselves. Christ said that our judgment is based on the way we treat the least of our brothers. When we visit the homeless, the sick, and the prisoners incarcerated in our jails, we visit and befriend Jesus.

The government is slowly getting out of social programs because in many cases they have done more harm than good and because they represent an ever increasing burden on taxpayers. Maybe that's the way it should be. If we Christians don't respond to the legitimate needs of the needy, we'll have chaos in our society and even greater social injustice. Are you as a Christian more concerned with "three strikes and you're out" for criminals, or are you more concerned about children born into poverty? Do you vote your pocketbook, or do you vote the Gospel?

I don't say this to create guilt, but these persistent social ills are problems we must deal with. Ask yourself: What would I give up to help the poor? It's easy to do the talk, much harder to walk the walk. I found this was true with myself when I saw those pictures of starving kids in Somalia. I wanted the government to intervene. Then I asked myself, "Would I give up a vacation or have a hot dog instead of a steak so these kids could eat?"

As Christians we are called upon to convert, to live the Gospel in our daily lives. However, many of us want the poor to go away, and we pretend they don't exist. In his book, *History of Cultures in the World*, Arnold Toynbee states that every culture can be evaluated by how it treats its poorest members.

The deepest split in Christianity today is not between Catholic and Lutheran or Methodist and Episcopalian. Hopefully all of these religions will someday come together. Catholics will appreciate the scriptures more and the Protestants will better understand the sacraments. The real split lies in how we understand scripture. On one side we have scripture as interpretation, and on the other we have scripture as history, the fundamentalists. The two will never agree as long as they start from that opposing premise.

While we were taught fundamentalism in the past, today the Church no longer teaches it. We teach scripture not as history, but as an interpretation of an interpretation in which the author writes about his experience of God and communicates it to his community. He uses the world view, philosophies, and attitudes of his time to communicate his experience of God.

UNDERSTANDING SCRIPTURE

If we are to understand scripture, we must first comprehend it in terms of the society for which it was written and then interpret it in terms of our community today. Since the author is interpreting his experience of God for his community, we must interpret it for our community since scripture is an interpretation of an interpretation. There is a profound difference between this and understanding scripture as history, the way I was taught.

For example, if we were to examine the Babylonian epics for the creation story and the flood, which were written a thousand years before Genesis, it would become obvious that the author had this Babylonian account in front of him when he wrote the story of Genesis. The writings are nearly identical to the words in Genesis. What becomes important now isn't the history of it — what God created on each of the seven days — but how it is different from the Babylonian text.

In the Babylonian text there are many gods, and man is just above the animals. However, in the Jewish text there is only one God, and man was created in God's image. The author used a comparison of the text to communicate his experience of God.

In the New Testament, Paul, like the majority of men in his time, was a male chauvinist. Women were second-class citizens in the Greek, Roman, and Jewish worlds. Women were required to cover their heads and submit to their husbands. Paul was simply a man of his times, and that was his world view. His view has been passed on in Christianity.

I have several examples of this. As I've mentioned, my dad ran a large furniture business. He told me that when he furnished a parish in northern California, the pastor ordered the best mattress available for himself, while the nuns received the cheapest. I taught in Jesuit high schools and can tell you that there is a tremendous difference in prestige between the boys' high school and the girls'. It used to be that in a meeting with both men and women if a man said something intelligent, I expected it; if a woman did, I was surprised. That was my prejudice for many years.

However, we find with Mormons, Jehovah's Witnesses, Baptists, and other fundamentalists that men are always the head of the house because that's how it's written in scriptures. I will not perform a wedding in which the couple chooses the reading, "Woman, obey your husband in all things possible." Today the man is not the head of the home, but rather it's a partnership of shared wisdom. Each brings wisdom to the relationship.

Paul says that alcoholism is a moral issue; yet, we've discovered that it's a disease. I have known some Mormon bishops who wouldn't let their members enter *Alcoholics Anony-*

mous because scripture says it's a moral issue, and they should be able to handle the problem themselves. Yet this is not the core of what Paul was trying to communicate.

As with alcoholism, we have to look at homosexuality in light of the information available on the subject today. For centuries we presumed one's sexual orientation was a choice. Contrary to what the Bible says, science may discover that sexual orientation is not a matter of choice but rather genetic make-up. Regardless of what any of us think, we need to be open to what science tells us.

Paul writes that homosexuality is a moral choice, but so did everybody else in Paul's time. Many people believe Paul was divinely inspired, that he had wisdom and knowledge on all matters and for all ages. However, Paul's attitude was merely typical of his time. We can't go to Paul to learn how people become this way. I'm not talking about sexual behavior but about orientation. The thrust and importance of his writings are not on the immorality of homosexuality but on his experience of God. It is the life, death, and resurrection of Jesus that holds significance for each of us for all times.

Now we're ready to enter into the second difference in the model. Recall the way Christians of the medieval period created a specific place for everything. I discussed this earlier; yet, it's important we understand this aspect of the old model upon which the teachings were based. Events held significance because they could be seen and touched. Thus, the sacraments were all-important as they occurred on a certain day, at a specific place, and they could be seen. Heaven was placed in the sky because it was light, a characteristic of God. Hell was placed underneath the ground because it was dark and evil. Angels depicted the presence of good, and the devil represented the power of evil in the world. Everything was put into a specific place because that is how they understood the world at that time.

An influential model for the medieval Christians was the world of Saint Augustine. He held the view that when we came into life, everything was in order. When we put things out of order and sinned, we went down to hell. If we kept things in order, we went up to heaven. Life on earth was our trial period. The significance of Saint Augustine's influence is that it placed importance on the spatial.

Today we see things in terms of process, where the journey is more important than the results, where the event is only important if it celebrates something in the journey. The journey is an unseen, spiritual dimension, and we don't need to put it into space.

The phrase "live one day at a time" is a common expression that focuses our attention on the here and now in which the moment is embraced. Unfortunately, many of us — especially our younger people — place too much emphasis on events. When we live for weekends or vacations, we make events the source of life's meaning. However, it's our life that gives each event meaning. As I mentioned earlier, we either place our priority on the journey we are living or on the events that happen to us. In medieval days they emphasized the events. Today we are learning to emphasize the journey.

Thanksgiving, for example, has become an authentic holy day. It comes from the community and celebrates family. It's not imposed on us; it comes from us. It's an event that celebrates our journey. I was at a parish when we were fighting in the Gulf war. A mass was held for people to pray for our servicemen, and the church was packed. That was a holy day which was initiated by the community. The important reality is what happens to us on this unseen journey, and events are only important as they fit into the journey.

WE ARE THE BODY OF CHRIST

The third difference lies in our notion of church. Medieval Christians equated the Church with God. If there was a Catholic king, he put the Protestants to death; if he was Protestant, he killed the Catholics. This idea of the Church and God being one and the same persisted through the centuries and is still present in the beliefs of some Catholics today.

For me, I was implicitly taught there was no salvation outside the Church. When anybody died or was dying, I used to pray not that he find God but that he had been or would be baptized into the Church. I encounter that view in some Catholic parents today who are upset that their children are good Protestants. The Church is not God but a faith community subject to the same faults and imperfections as humans. A phenomena that has occurred in the last thirty years is that when people talk about the Church, they don't mean the Vatican or the chancery but their own parish.

There are conservative movements within the Church that view the Pope and Bishops as the Church, "apostolic succession." Since they cannot serve all the needs of the Church and parishioners themselves, priests and lay people fill in and assist in a subservient role to them.

While this may be a sensible way of looking at the Church, the movements don't reflect the meaning of Jesus nor hold up under scripture scholarship. Jesus came to create a faith community. He called on people like us as believers to carry his presence into the world. According to scripture scholars this is what Jesus meant by the term for church, ecclesia. However, every institution has to have authority for without it we would have chaos. Yet, this authority is not the Church, just as the federal government in Washington is not

America. Authority plays an important role within the institution of the Church, but it isn't the Church.

We are the Church.

I visited a parish in southern California where the priest said, "Body of Christ" during communion, and many parishioners responded, "Yes, we are." I found that inspiring. Every time they received communion, the parishioners affirmed they were the Body of Christ.

Today I see a separation in the Church between people who say they are Christians who have chosen to be Catholics and those who express they are Catholics who have chosen to be Christians. It's a matter of what is more important in our lives. Are we a person of God or are we primarily a person of the institutional Church? They don't have the same meaning.

I meet many different priests wherever I go, and I perceive a considerable difference between whether they are men of God first or men of the Church. I don't worship the Church. I worship in the Church.

While our notion of church has changed from medieval times, we still need to remind ourselves that the Church consists of imperfect humans and can become confused at times. It can have dark periods as well as growing experiences just as human beings do. The Church is not a perfect institution but one that changes and evolves through time.

A good example of how the Church endures in human dimension is in our devotion to Mary. As children many of us were brought up with the notion of a God who was very distant and strict. The idea of a God who would send me to hell for all eternity for missing mass once on Sunday, a God so ready to punish me wasn't a personal God with whom I felt comfortable sharing my life. He wasn't all that nice. How were we to approach such a God? Well, we would go through Mary, and she would intercede for us. During May and October Mary was more important to me than God because at mass we didn't go to attend mass but to say the rosary.

This ritual was an established way of communicating with God. It seemed we had more devotion to Mary than we did to God. Even as a Jesuit I was taught to pray to Mary, and she would go to God for us. This accepted practice is part of our Church's history because God was held far and distant from us. As I mentioned earlier we become the god we worship. In our devotion to Mary many families become like that. There may be a dad who is hard to approach. He may be a good, just and fair man, but one who is self-righteous, difficult to talk to, and who always says no. Consequently, we go to mom and she approaches dad with our request. This is certainly not an ideal model.

When I first studied scripture and began to understand the words of Jesus, I realized that Jesus didn't come to bring us to a relationship with Mary. There is nothing in the scripture that tells us that. Jesus came to bring us to the Father within, to a personal relationship with God. My devotion to Mary was replaced with the recognition that Mary's gift to us from God is that of surrender . . . "Be it done unto me according to thy will." She is a perfect example of what all of us are trying to live — God's will.

If we reflect on Mary, we can see that throughout her life she had to trust God, and that must have been terribly difficult at times. Mary was human, not God. She was just like us. Imagine it is the golden jubilee of the parish and thousands were in attendance along with many Bishops. How would a mother feel if she lost her twelve-year-old one Sunday and didn't know where he went. Imagine the panic, the self-recrimination. Think what would race through her mind when she at last finds him in the rectory lecturing the Bishops about God.

Mary saw that Jesus wasn't normal and surely was bothered by it, but she accepted. "Be it done unto me according to Thy will." Mary went through a process of surrender. Why did she accept? Because she had so much faith that God was with her.

What do you want for your son? A nice girl, family, a home, a good job, and you hope that he stays out of trouble. Jesus had none of this. Reflect that Mary was a Jewish mother and surely wanted grandchildren. She had to have harbored that desire for her son, who was such a wonderful, caring, and loving human being to marry and have children, but her Jesus was a person who wandered from town to town without a place to lay his head. She must have heard the threatening warnings, the people talking about putting him to death. The people who taught her in temple on the Sabbath were the same men who wanted her son dead. This was not easy. Surely she struggled with her faith for she could not like much of what she saw happening to her son. As I said, her trust in God was surely tested many times.

One of the most moving aspects of my Catholic faith is Mary at the foot of the cross. It is so hard to lose a child. Visualize the scene of Mary and Jesus saying goodbye to each other at the cross, one of the most beautiful images in our Christian faith. He didn't just die, but died as a common criminal between two thieves. However, she had to let him go, unaware of what any of this meant. She had to trust God completely; yet, it couldn't have been easy for her. She must have struggled with it as we would have. "Be it done unto me according to thy will."

Mary's great gift to us today is her example of surrender, of saying yes to God. She accepted what was happening because she had faith that God was with her. She showed us how to reach God, how to accept, how to say "yes." Mary is an important part of our devotion. Our understanding of her as our bridge from our old notion of a distant God to a personal one, it is an understanding that has evolved through time.

My hardest cross in life is my desire to create the world in my image. I find it very hard to go with the flow. Mary is a gift from God to show me how to let go, to get to God. She is as important to me today as she ever was.

The final difference is philosophical. Thomas Aquinas defined man as a rational animal who was separated from other living creatures by his ability to reason. Aquinas's rational animal definition is very individualistic and promotes a relationship solely between God and me. Consequently, we developed a morality that exists just between God and me.

The emphasis was on personal sin rather than sin within the community, such as sins of gossip or prejudice, acts that dealt with other people. Even the churches built then were long and narrow like football fields, and services were conducted in Latin. It didn't matter because the relationship was just between me and God.

✝

Today we define man as relational. Our uniqueness comes from our ability to love and be loved. In the modern model we define our relationship as we to God. Some of the churches architecturally built today are more community oriented.

This is a great challenge for Catholics. When I go to a Protestant church, friendly people will greet me, introduce themselves, thank me for coming, invite me for coffee, and urge me to return the next week. No one does the same in a Catholic church. I can go to mass, go to communion, and no one will speak to me. However, I have noticed in recent years that many parishes are now making an effort to welcome worshipers.

Chapter Eleven

THE SACRAMENTS

11

The sacraments should be a bridge between our personal experience of God and our experience as a Christian community. Unfortunately, many Catholics view the sacraments as archaic and without meaning. The sacraments celebrate significant events within our spiritual journey. They come from within the spiritual community instead of being imposed upon the community. While the sacraments are steeped in tradition, they do indeed play a vital role in our spiritual development and expression.

The different aspects I have just discussed characterize the views of the Church in which many of us were raised. They represent two different world views. Understanding how the Church has changed, we can find new meaning in the sacraments. We need to see them as significant events, but if people put all the meaning into the event, they will view the sacraments as magic that doesn't make any sense in today's world. We cannot afford to view the sacraments from a model that was relevant in medieval times but no longer works.

A sacrament, by definition, is a sign instituted by Christ to give grace. What exactly is meant by the term "grace?" When we are around very special friends, we feel differently than we normally do. They bring something out that is within us, but only with them does it emerge. Even if we haven't seen them in years, we can talk with them as if we saw them yesterday.

God's love is always with us. A "grace experience" is one in which we feel the experience of God when we're around it. This event — this sacrament — has brought to our awareness the presence of God in our lives.

As a priest I strive to find relevance in everything I do. I never try to preach or live in a manner I don't believe in. It is essential that the sacraments mean what they say. Otherwise, our performance of them will merely contribute to the irrelevance of church in our lives.

The sacrament celebrates what is happening in the human journey. The importance should be placed on the journey itself while the sacraments are special events that celebrate the journey. In the medieval world the events were all-important, so the sacraments, rather than the journey, were all-important.

BAPTISM

In the old days infants were baptized as soon as possible after birth because of our notion of original sin. In my case I was baptized in a hospital incubator because I was born six weeks early, and it was thought I would die. In fact, my mom promised God that if I lived, I would be a priest! In those days it was believed that if children died and weren't baptized, they went to limbo. Even today grandmothers sneak up on their grandchildren if the parents haven't baptized their children, and manage to sprinkle water over their heads, and utter the words of baptism. In some cultures parents will rush their newborns to the church as soon as they get home from the hospital, believing that once the water is poured over the child's head, the baby becomes a child of God. Someone, especially the younger generation, could easily view this as magic because all the significance is put on the event.

Today many parishes won't baptize a child if the parents don't attend church or don't live the Christian faith. This is a cause of stress in some families. Grandparents become alarmed and upset because their grandchildren aren't baptized.

The meaning of baptism is that the love of the parents for each other goes from the parents to the child. Baptism is a rite of initiation and is for the awareness of the parents. If we don't intend to live the faith in the Church, why be baptized? Baptism takes away original sin, but how do we understand original sin? In the old model everything was placed in the event. The ritual of baptism washed away original sin. Today we see the ritual as a sign that the parents' unconditional love for each other is shared with the child. This process takes away original sin, the result of conditional love. Today we say that the child is introduced into the Christian way of life through the parents.

We develop the hunger for God's love by first experiencing the wonder of parental love. The way the parents show forgiveness and unconditional love plants the seeds of God's love in their children.

Baptism is a sign that expresses initiation into this process. It is a very special event for parents and not one whose meaning is limited to Catholics. The Church recognizes baptism in any Christian denomination because we're baptized into the Christian life.

CONFIRMATION

Confirmation is when we affirm that we want to live the Christian life in the Catholic church. I was confirmed in the seventh grade — we all were because Sister Elizabeth Louise wouldn't let any of us get out of it. I remember being afraid the Bishop might ask me what the Fruits of the Holy Spirit were or one of those other questions we had to study and memorize. Some of us older Catholics can remember those days.

When I made my confirmation, I promised I would never see an R-rated movie nor drink until I turned twenty-one. At that time I was just entering the age of concupiscence, and I needed the grace of this sacrament to battle the devil.

Today we confirm people in their junior or senior year of high school, and I still think that's too early. In our culture we give our young people plenty of freedom but little responsibility. Adolescents can be confirmed one week, and the next week they may declare they will never to go to church again.

Confirmation is a very personal sacrament. It should take place when a person first believes in his heart the good news of Jesus Christ, when he discovers how much God loves him, and how much God's love is within him. That's when a person becomes an adult Christian and is ready to make a commitment. That is the time to celebrate.

Confirmation is an adult decision, a celebration of discovery. Like all the sacraments, it is a celebration of something that happens, a key moment in our journey with God. It is a moment that occurs at a different time in each one of our journeys. For some it may come as they lie on their death bed while for others it could be associated with their marriage. However, that moment is too beautiful and momentous for us to push on a young person simply because the child has reached a certain age.

The significance of confirmation is that it means what it says. I've talked about Protestants understanding better than Catholics that faith is a decision. Confirmation is a realization that faith is based on this decision. It is when we realize we are a child of God and born again. When someone has made the decision to lead a spiritual life, that should be the time for a coming together of the community to celebrate this decision and administer the sacrament of confirmation.

RECONCILIATION

There is still some confusion today among many Catholics regarding the sacrament of reconciliation. Many of us were taught as children that we had to go to confession in order to gain God's forgiveness and to receive communion. Many Catholics still believe they are obliged to go at least once a year.

Today the name has been changed (we no longer call it confession), and the rules have changed too. Now we only have to go to the sacrament if we've done something seriously wrong. There is no yearly obligation.

All of us sin, and all of us are capable of committing serious sins. The medieval world thought of sin in physical terms, so we put sin in events. Certain events, for example, disobeying a parent or stealing, were sinful.

We sin when we go through periods in our life when we're filled with self-pity, hatred, or a feeling of worthlessness because sin is not letting God love us. Sin is living in darkness, and all of us are capable of that.[1]

All of us are sinners and all of us have had times when we were self-centered and preoccupied with ourselves. We don't pull out of it until we grow sick and tired of being sick and tired. Nobody, including God, can help us if we're not ready or receptive. We have to bottom out on blaming other people and making excuses. We have to realize our misery is between God and ourselves to fix. We have to take responsibility for the fact that we are sinners. We must remember that conversion is a process that occurs over many months, not in a single moment of insight. If we seek to get rid of sin, we are ridding ourselves of conscience. Sin is the process, not the events that result. This is not to say that the events are not bad or to be condemned. They are.

---

[1] I am not talking about clinical depression. I have noticed over the years that certain people carry a heaviness that is always with them. It's not something they've chosen. It's the physiological makeup of their body.

God's love is unconditional. If we believe this and let God forgive us, we can forgive ourselves. If we don't bring God's forgiveness into our sinfulness, we'll spring right back into the dark hole and feel worse than before. We become upset because we've been so preoccupied with ourselves and, consequently, wind up even more wrapped up in ourselves. Forgiveness is essential. It's part of this conversion.

The only sin that God cannot forgive is the sin against the Spirit, that is, when we refuse God's love and forgiveness. God does not force his love or forgiveness on any of us. God respects our freedom. God will let us feel as bad about ourselves as we want to feel. God will let us stay guilty throughout our entire lives if that is what we want.

The way I try to understand God's forgiveness is by remembering how I felt after a general confession when I was in the fifth grade. I was walking across the street and thought I'd go straight to heaven if I died at that moment. As I believed then is how I should always believe as a Christian. God's love and forgiveness are a gift. This is why pride is a rejection of God's love. We place ourselves as god, believing we must earn God's forgiveness.

When we go to the sacrament of reconciliation, we don't go to be forgiven because we're already forgiven. We go to the sacrament to celebrate God's unconditional love and acceptance. When something wonderful has happened in our lives, we celebrate it. Reconciliation is a sacrament of celebration.

I've spent many hours listening to people in the confessional, and this sacrament has been one of my greatest joys, as well as one of my greatest sorrows. It fills me with faith when people come in brimming with God's joy in their hearts. They've truly discovered the Father's love, and they're celebrating it. However, it's so sad when people come in and confess they've missed mass on Sunday because they were sick. I can only wonder what kind of god they have.

It has been my experience that, unfortunately, some people use the sacrament of reconciliation as a substitute for faith. They go to the sacrament not to celebrate God's forgiveness but to make sure they are doing everything right in order to gain entrance to heaven. This way of thinking is self-centered; it's not God-centered. These people are convinced that they are the ones who must do everything right. They won't let go and allow God to love them.

There is also another significant aspect to reconciliation. During my years at St. Francis in Phoenix, Arizona, I spent many hours a week hearing confessions. People came in to not only celebrate God's forgiveness but also to share their problems and struggles. This kind of spiritual direction plays an important role in this sacrament.

We all need people to help us in our spiritual journey. If we are to stay honest and continue to grow, each one of us needs a spiritual director, someone we allow to challenge us.

Another beauty of the sacrament is that it gives us the freedom to name our sins. When I heard confession for grade school children, I thought it was a marvelous opportunity for them because it was probably the only time during the year when they ever said something was their fault. Usually it was the teacher's fault or a brother's or sister's fault. Reconciliation is a time when we can honestly say, "It is my fault." Once we admit it, we can grow.

We must realize we're in a period of transition. The old has died, but the new hasn't fully arrived. In the Church that is emerging, the sacrament of reconciliation will be one of the most important. It's a beautiful time of coming together, of celebrating God's love and forgiveness in our lives, and receiving spiritual direction in our journey.

THE EUCHARIST

The Eucharist alone would take a whole book to examine properly. All I can do is address a few points. Catholics have to believe as a matter of faith that Jesus is really present in the Eucharist. How we explain this presence depends on the model we use. The medievalist explained everything in physical terms so the meaning was in Jesus who was present in the Eucharist and became physically present during the words of consecration. We called this "transubstantiation." For a long time the only importance the Church placed in the Eucharist was receiving communion. It didn't matter how we sang, how important the sermon was, or what language the mass was in. All that was important was that we receive communion, and tremendous emphasis was given to physically receiving the Body and Blood of Jesus Christ.

This again dates back to the medieval need to interpret everything in space and form. Some of us may recall it was a sin if our teeth touched the host. If the host fell, how the priest would sprinkle holy water to cleanse the floor. Historically the emphasis was placed on the physical presence of the host, and our Catholic faith rested on this one reality of receiving communion.

It's interesting that on Holy Thursday, the day on which the Church celebrates the institution of the Eucharist, the Gospel is not the Gospel of the institution but is of the washing of feet. In the first ten chapters of John's Gospel, Jesus tries to teach the Jewish people, especially the leaders, about how much God loves them, but they hardened their hearts. So Jesus turns to his apostles to teach them how much God loves them. The first thing he does is get on his knees and wash their feet, a function performed in Jewish society by servants.

Never before in a religion had a God been presented as a servant. Notice how Peter reacts. "Oh no, Lord! Let me wash your feet!" Jesus says to Peter, "Unless you let me wash your feet, you cannot be my disciple." Unless we let God love us, we have nothing to give away. Then Jesus turned to his apostles. "As I have washed your feet, you are to do this for one another." That has always been for me the significance of what Jesus had in mind for his Church.

Therefore, as a Church we must place greater importance on the need to connect the Eucharist with the way we conduct our lives. Receiving communion is not the apex of being a Christian or Catholic. The apex is living the Christian life. We come to church and celebrate this in the Eucharist.

We also come to the Eucharist to receive strength and to celebrate our faith so that we can go forth and live our faith in our communities and in our families. The Church is a community of believers who unite together as Christians, living together in the celebration of the Eucharist.

What we need in the Church today is this aspect of a faith-filled community, people who are living their faith in their daily lives. We can't settle on being Christians only on Sunday when we go to church. We must make our time at church a celebration of how we live every day. This is something we have to work at day by day, one step at a time.

Some parishes are trying to nurture this celebration of faith by building small communities within their parish. It's been an interesting experience of mine that the greatest masses I've ever presided over as a priest have been family masses. A family is after all the closest of communities.

MATRIMONY

Sometimes I wake up in the middle of the night concerned by the thought that over half of the seven hundred marriages I've performed are invalid as sacraments. This anxiety stems from my perception that too many couples simply aren't ready to enter this sacrament.

It generally takes people a long time to grow up in our culture. I know many people who finally discovered what a marriage is after their third try. We live in a world where our daily lives are filled with stress, where we're engulfed with material distractions that divert attention from connecting with our inner self. Many young people fall in love; yet, they haven't developed their spiritual lives. Not only do they lack an experience of God in their lives, but they often don't even have an experience of church. They're just two kids who are lonely and have found each other. They think they've found a god, a person who will make them happy the rest of their lives, and they want to marry that god.

That's not a sacrament. We make it a magic rite when we think that a marriage is made simply because a couple comes to the altar and exchanges vows. The sacrament can only celebrate what we've already achieved.

We must remember that the journey is a process. It's never perfect, and we never reach an end. Before we can ever have a sense of God in our lives, we must have a sense of self, a sense of knowing who we are. I can always tell if the marriage is a sacrament or not by observing whether the groom or bride minimizes himself (or herself) and maximizes the other. That means they have made the other person their god, and that's not a sacrament. We need to maximize ourselves because it's our own experience of God inside that makes a relationship meaningful. Without this sense of self we are unable to make a permanent commitment.

Some of the best marriages I've witnessed are with couples who married when they were in their early thirties. They have an idea of who they are. They've had an experience of God in their lives, and they're ready to make this decision. It's a faith experience. The sacrament of marriage celebrates how they live and how they've made the commitment.

Every time I perform a wedding that has no spiritual core — I'm doing it to please parents or to make everybody happy — I'm helping the Church become a museum. This is one of my struggles as a priest.

When I was ordained into the priesthood, I didn't really know what it meant to be a priest. It wasn't until about seven years after my ordination that I truly understood the priesthood.

When I perform weddings about which I'm doubtful, I say a silent prayer and hope that someday these marriages will become a sacrament. Indeed couples often experience the sacrament of marriage years after they've gone through the ceremony.

And bear in mind an all-too-common misunderstanding about annulment. It doesn't mean it wasn't a marriage. Annulment means the marriage was never a sacrament.

Another dilemma I face is with the many young couples who want to be married but have quit going to church. Many parishes will not marry a couple who have been away from the Church. The Church handles this dilemma by establishing a six-month waiting period before marriage. I feel if we slam the door on these couples, we will never see them again. In these situations I try to teach the couples about the sacraments, update their faith, and work with them in love and kindness. By doing so I hope that someday these couples will remember how they were treated and come back to the Church.

Too often we forget couples after they are married. I don't think couples listen to much of what's said by others before they marry. Most couples I marry are in love, and anything I tell them doesn't hold any great importance. The divorce rate among Catholics is basically the same as for society in general. If we as a faith community are going to hold to the integrity of the sacrament, we have to concern ourselves with our young people after they marry, before they get caught up in the materialism and externalism of our society. This would be a great mission for our Catholic couples who have made it work. After the wedding is when we as a community need to be supportive and help young couples work through their difficulties. The Church should spend more energy and place more importance on what happens after marriage.

The sacraments are not events that cause a spiritual awakening or magically create a spiritual connection with our inner self and God. They're ceremonies that celebrate what we've already discovered — God's unconditional love.

The sacraments are a bridge between our spirituality and our religion. Without a faith and acceptance of the source of that unconditional love, the sacraments are meaningless rites that carry no relevance in our lives. On the other hand, once we accept the good news of Jesus Christ, the sacraments become rites of celebration that breathe life into our religion and can transform our Church into a faith community.

Chapter Twelve

PRAYER

12

If we're going to understand prayer, we must try to understand God as much as we are capable of understanding him. Prayer is the way we stay connected to God. What makes Christianity different from other religious beliefs is our belief in the Trinity. Yet, for the most part we know little about it.

I often speak of Father-centered spirituality, the kingdom within us all. Yet, I have heard people talk about this same reality and call it Jesus Christ. I've heard others identify it as the Holy Spirit. If someone were to come from Mars and listen to Christians speak about God, they could easily think we believe in three different Gods.

One of the problems with fundamentalism is the inherent belief that Jesus came to bring us to a relationship with Jesus. Jesus came to bring us to the Father, to the love we carry inside. We strive to be Christ-like as we approach the Father within. Too many people get stuck on Jesus and never get to the Father. Also while the charismatic community has been an important development in the Church, some charismatics become so wrapped up in the Spirit that they fail to connect and root it to the Father within. Consequently, when dealing with problems that beset their lives, they are overwhelmed.

The Trinity is not "the" mystery. The great Christian mystery is how much God loves us. God's love is always a mystery, and we'll never understand why it is inexhaustible. No matter how far we fall, God's love is always there; it is never exhausted within us. Not only is God's love a mystery but also is the love of one person for another. This love is much more than what they feel for one another. It is more than what they do for one another. It is more than their personalities or their looks. If you try to prove and test love, you destroy it. Love is a mystery we should accept.

In order to understand prayer we need to understand the Trinity and recognize it as the core of our spiritual experience. Without this understanding, the Trinity becomes yet one more intellectual concept without any real meaning.

Today we say there are three persons in one God — Father, Son and Spirit. The word "person" doesn't mean a separate physical body or entity. It meant "characteristic" as defined in the Fifth Century. Some of us may recall the use of masks which identified comedies and tragedies in our literature books. Comedies used the mask with a smile; in tragedies, the mask bore a frown. These masks expressed the characteristic or mood of the play. When we say there are three persons in one God, we mean there are three characteristics to the experience of God, and all three of these must be present.

THE FATHER

The first characteristic is what Jesus asked us to call Father. It is the love inside of us, the kingdom within. Each one of us possesses the personality of God. In most people I have come to know, I've discovered their primary motivation is to love and be loved. This drive comes from God. The people who discover what life is all about are those who realize that God is love. When we talk about what binds us together in our families, marriages, and friendships, we're speaking about God. Whenever we talk about God, we speak of love, the love that is inside each of us.

As new-borns and young children, we're innocent and filled with love. This love that's so accepting soon becomes obscured. We grow up in family environments of conditional love where like some genetic carrier earned love is passed from generation to generation.

In our corporate society today the father is often not a significant part of the family equation. If fathers aren't absent because of divorce or abandonment, many of them are not at home by choice. They may be well intentioned but are too preoccupied with finding their meaning in the corporate world. With no extended family to assist in taking care of the children, the mother is often the one left with the task of raising the family. Again and again this situation results in financial and emotional strain. The meaning of life is no longer as paramount as mere survival — just making it through.

Emerson wrote that most people live lives of "quiet desperation." As a consequence, we develop from the outside. This precious gift of love inside us remains hidden, undiscovered, and untapped. Instead of living from within and believing we're precious, we react to outside forces and think that by being perfect, by doing and saying the right things, people will love us. We seek love and acceptance from others by altering our behavior. We never connect with the source of love within, the love that is there that need not be earned. We continue to look for love "in all the wrong places."

Many fundamentalists fail to understand the real meaning of the scriptures and try to make them God. The scriptures are a love letter from God to us. We don't worship the scriptures. I tell people not to quote them to me. Instead I ask that they share their life with me. I can look the scriptures up for myself. Likewise, some make the Church God. I find the same reality in twelve-step programs that I have found in religion. Some people make the twelve-step program their god and never find a personal God. The name we have for this is co-dependency: people who try to find meaning on the outside. These are people who are co-dependent on co-dependency and make their program god. Every time a book comes out, they have to read it. They attend workshops to find the latest answer. They make these meetings and therapies their god. They've made the problem the never-ending answer to their life's troubles.

We train our young people through music and films that there is a right person out there, that happiness is a matter of meeting that person, and when we meet the right person; we'll get married, have children, and live happily ever after.

That isn't the way it works because the right person is within us.

How sad it is when I see high school and even elementary school students walking around without realizing they carry the gift of God's love. They think they must earn love. They feel they have to get straight A's, make the football team, or win an elected position on the student council. This process continues as they grow up. They feel they must earn a college degree, have a big house, or hold some highly esteemed job.

We mistakenly accept that what gives us value is what we do and what we amass. Society reinforces this every day of our lives. This gift of love remains always present but sealed behind a wall of what we feel we must do or be. We walk through life pretending we're perfect and expecting others to be perfect in turn.

That is our great sin. We ignore and refuse to accept God's love, which Jesus asks us to call Father. This love inside us is the first characteristic of the Trinity.

Let me anthropomorphise for a moment. That means make God like a human being so we can understand the mind of God. I love playing God. I'm up in my heaven, and I look out at all the people I've created out of love. Everyone's talking; no one's listening. They're all going in different directions. I want to speak to my people, to tell them the way I created them to be. Jesus Christ becomes the word from God to us. He was the living example of the way God created us to live.

THE SON

When I took a film class, the teacher said to always notice the first image on the screen and the last image. That will tell you the theme. Let's look at Jesus. The first image we have is the stable, the last is the cross. Why the stable? Why the cross? Because Jesus was born in humble circumstances and because the way we find God is through pain and suffering.

When I was a young Jesuit, I thought Jesus died on the cross so I didn't have to suffer on the cross. But in reality Jesus was showing me that I have to die on the "cross" to reach the "resurrection." He was showing me the way.

This path, therefore, is not one characterized by our perfection or successes. These things merely inflate our egos. Instead we discover God when we carry our personal cross, when we stumble and fall, when we're in the desert. Jesus had to go through his cross to get to his resurrection, and each of us must go through our cross to reach our resurrection.

Have we ever known a winning army to surrender? It's when we count our losses and face the pain that we have need for God. We don't go to God when we're on a winning streak but when we're knocked to our knees. We must discover in our own way and in our own time the illusions and disillusionments of seeking our happiness in the false gods of our lives.

I've counseled many people, and I have seen so much pain, so much suffering. It is my hope and sincere desire that each one of us comes to realize that our worth does not come from our husband, wife or kids, but from the love — the free gift of love — we carry inside us. When that begins to dawn on each of us, we then come to understand the second characteristic of the experience of God. Jesus brings us to the kingdom within, the good news of our salvation. It is this love within that keeps us going through dark times. It is this love that eventually gets us moving again after we've experienced tragedy.

For me, as I travel, the road can become long and lonely. What keeps me going is the individual who comes up to me, grabs my hand on his way out, and says, "Father, you don't know what this week has meant to me." Maybe he has lived his life controlled by a god of punishment and had felt deep within he did not have a chance. Suddenly, he realizes God loves him. He has accepted the Gospel of Jesus.

THE SPIRIT

Once we truly accept his kingdom of love within us, an inner transformation, a conversion, takes place on our human journey. We become reborn and truly baptized in the Spirit. We become the god we worship, and we give away to others the love and forgiveness God has given to us. We show others the compassion God has shown us.

Charity isn't something we do. Being charitable is something we are and comes from inside. The Spirit of God flows through us to others. Jesus said, "By their fruits you shall know them." People who have it give it away.

I said earlier that I don't trust anyone who speaks about God who is not compassionate. Love and kindness are the signs of God's presence. It's through brokenness and sinfulness that we discover we're vehicles of God's love, and it's this love that transforms us into compassionate and forgiving people. Jesus gave us one commandment — to "love one another as I have loved you." That's living the life of the Spirit, and it comes from God's love within us.

The Trinity then consists of three characteristics: the Father as the kingdom of love within us; the Son as Jesus Christ, the Way, who brings us to the Father; and the Spirit — the moving force that allows God's love and power to flow through us to others. This is my experience of the Trinity.

TYPES OF PRAYER

With this understanding of the Trinity, the act of prayer takes on a very important and relevant meaning. Prayer is essential if we are to grow spiritually. The process of praying is eminently important because this is the way we stay connected to the love inside, the Father.

All I've written before comes together through prayer. Time spent in prayer is the most important spiritual tool we nurture. I would like to share six types of prayer, ways I stay connected to the love inside me on a daily basis. The first of these is what I call a centering prayer.

The first thing I do when I wake up in the morning is to decide when I will pray that day. If I don't make it the most important act of the day, then I never get around to praying. I have found that whatever I make most important is what I end up doing.

Every day I spend about a half hour walking on the beach or in some quiet neighborhood. I used to jog when I was younger. When I was in Phoenix, I climbed Squaw Peak and called it my "prayer mountain." I usually wait until the afternoon because by then I have plenty of problems that have accumulated throughout the day. During my walk I offer to God all the things that are bothering me — anger, anxieties, fears, and guilt that I feel inside.

As mentioned, spirituality is developing reactions to our reactions. Prayer is where I bring God's love into my reactions. After I've messed up and I'm berating myself is when I ask God to teach me how to grow from it. When I have a problem accepting something about life, I ask Mary to help me let go so I can say, "Be it done unto me according to Thy will." When I have deep anger towards someone I ask God to remove it from me.

I take each problem one at a time and examine each one trying to discern their source and nature. If I have a problem with somebody else, I try to get underneath that person's skin to find the source of the problem. I quiet my mind and listen with an open heart. God exists within us, and if we really listen, God will speak to our hearts.

When I talk about God speaking within us, I mean there is an inner truth or presence. This presence is an in dwelling of the Spirit. The voice is not literal, and we must be open to perceive it. Often when people have a problem, they will walk along the shore or in the woods, and these settings will calm them. It is when we have that kind of inner peace that we hear this intuitive voice.

Many people don't hear God speaking because they go to God with the answer; they listen with an agenda. They just want God to agree with them. Many times I hear what I don't want to hear, but I always hear what I need to hear.

When I was first introduced to prayer I was taught to rid myself of distractions. In centering, I make my distractions the prayer. We tend to neglect or bury the things that bother us when those are the very things we need to pray about. I may have many things on my mind, but I take one problem at a time and listen until I receive an answer. That is how I stay connected; this is where I really work on honesty with myself. This centering prayer is the cornerstone of my spirituality.

An example of a problem resolved through prayer centered on an occurrence with my dad a year before he died. I had planned to take my parents on a two-day trip, but I needed to have my car repaired. Since the mechanic would be working on the rear of the vehicle, I was concerned that my video and audio cassette tapes would be immersed in grease. I asked my mom if I could stack them in their storeroom across the street from their house. As I was getting the keys, dad said, "Son, what are you going to do?" I told him that I was going to stack my tapes in his storeroom.

"There isn't enough room," he said. I found out he was right, but I went ahead and placed them in the entrance way to the storeroom. My dad saw what I'd done and approached me, quite upset.

"Suppose I want to go fishing?" he protested. His fishing equipment was in the back of the storeroom and my dad hadn't gone fishing in five years, so I dismissed his objection.

I went back to the house and left my dad at the storeroom. He pouted all day over the incident. I also was miserable.

I had this fear that he would have a heart attack, and it would be my fault. The altercation bothered us as we both sat in the living room in a heavy silence. So that afternoon I brought the incident to prayer. When I have a problem and take it to prayer, I apply a teaching of my mother. I often say that my Dad taught me to be a Catholic, my Mom taught me to be a Christian. She told me never to judge others until I walked in their shoes. This is what I did in my prayer that day. What I heard was very clear... "This is your Dad's house. You come in and intrude. You think you can come here and store things without even asking?"

After my prayer, I approached my Dad. "I have to talk to you," I said. "I'm sorry. I didn't even ask you this morning. I just went and acted like it was my house. It's not my house. It's your house. I understand, Dad, and I'm really sorry."

He stood up, came over, and hugged me. There were tears in his eyes. He said, "Son, forgive me. I acted just like a baby."

In the old days we both would have gone to bed that night without saying a word, and my Mom would have suffered the most. None of us would have slept very well. Later my Dad and I eventually would have started to "thaw" and communicate again, but the incident would have remained with us, carefully recorded in our black books.

Most people go outside to solve their problems. They turn to food, booze, or drugs; or they blame others, project on them, and rationalize. They seldom bring their problems to God. When I did not deal with my problems on a daily basis, I buried them. Consequently, they piled up inside me, and then I either exploded or became moody. This prayer has helped me become responsible for my feelings and my problems.

Prayer is the way I stay connected to God. When I don't take the time to pray, that's when the fast feet take over. Like a chicken with its head cut off, I become compulsive and disconnected. Without this connection within I can't be spiritual, and in its absence the external world assumes control. No matter how busy we are in our professions if we take the time to stay connected, we'll do a much better job with life. We'll be better husbands, wives, fathers, mothers, and friends.

We can only love somebody to the extent we know them. Prayer is letting God know us so that God can love us. When I was younger, I never let God know my problems. I spent much of my life emotionally and spiritually running away. Prayer is believing there is a God who cares. Through prayer we deal with our issues, stay connected, and ground ourselves.

When I take the time to be connected as I do in this first prayer, to rid myself of distractions, I am open to the second form of prayer. Most people can't reach the second form because they never rid themselves of their distractions.

The second type of prayer is living life in the moment. I call it the "sacrament of the moment." In the Old Testament Yahweh says, "I am who am." The meaning of this statement is significant for it conveys God is here in the present moment. Yesterday is history, and tomorrow is always a mystery.

I practice this prayer, this sacrament of the moment, by being where I'm supposed to be and doing what I'm supposed to do. We know how gratifying it feels when we talk to a person who gives us his full attention and makes us feel as if we're the most important person in the world. How lonely we feel when someone is preoccupied. Now is the most important moment in our lives because it is in this moment when life is really happening.

A friend of mine used to take me to the airport. He would pick me up, and then on the way to the airport, he would tell me he had to go to the post office. After the post office we would drop by the bank. Then he would stop at a convenience store for cigarettes. By the time we reached the airport, I was a nervous wreck. Now I tell him that I'll take a cab. I want somebody who will take me to the airport without squeezing more into the moment. A person who tries to do everything ends up accomplishing nothing.

A few years ago I gave a twelve-step retreat. A few of the participants warned me ahead of time about this one individual. "Father, he can't stay sober," one of them said. "He stays sober for a couple of months, and then he gets drunk again." They didn't know why. After the retreat I knew why. He skipped one of the conferences on Saturday to go watch his son play football. Then he left two of the conferences on Sunday because he wanted to watch the 49'ers play football. He never did what he was supposed to. He did three or four other things. When we go on a retreat, we should make a retreat.

Several years ago I was giving a mission in Seattle, Washington. The parish was filled with solicitous people concerned about how I was doing. "Are you OK?" they asked. "Are you satisfied with the turnout?" I no longer ask myself those questions. I just get up each day and do what I'm supposed to do and be where I'm supposed to be, and it all works.

My third type of prayer is one many of us do on a daily basis but perhaps aren't aware we're praying. I do it all the time. I used to think it was senility, but I've learned it's sanctity. I talk to myself. I find myself talking while walking down the street or driving a car. This monologue is my conscious contact with God.

I share with God my opinions of people, my deepest thoughts, things I would never share with anybody else. Every morning while I shower, I talk to God about the things I want to accomplish that day and what the day may have in store. A few years ago I moved back to my parents' home. It's humorous when I recall my mother approaching me one morning and asking, "Tom, I hear you talking in the morning when I pass your room. Who are you talking to in the shower?"

My fourth type of prayer is a prayer of praise. In the past I have always praised the Lord. Now I praise God in other people. When I compliment, extend my thanks to, or appreciate other people, I'm praising God because it's God's love within them that makes them so precious.

A few years ago when I arrived at a parish, several priests mentioned to me that the cook was not very good, that I was not to expect very good meals. However, during my two weeks there, the meals were excellent. The first Saturday night there I experienced a delicious, tender leg of lamb dinner. After the meal I made a special effort to compliment the cook. She probably hadn't had a compliment in years.

If others don't appreciate us, why should we make the effort? Jesus cured the ten lepers, and only one came back to say, "Thank you." Jesus asked where the other nine were. Even Jesus needed to be appreciated.

A fifth type of prayer involves the rosary. As a child and through my years as a young Jesuit, I endeavored to make the rosary meaningful. However, I developed headaches as I tried to meditate on the mystery while reciting the words at the same time. Eventually I gave up.

Yet, today the rosary is a very important part of my prayer life. I use it when I have one of those emotional days when I'm so upset and anxious I can't center my thoughts and reach God. Like a mantra (in which Eastern practitioners continually repeat a sound until their minds are free of thoughts), I use the rosary in a similar way to calm my emotions.

After reflecting for a moment on the mystery in the life of Mary or Jesus, I recite the rosary prayers without thinking about anything. I center myself on the Father inside me until I calm down. The number of decades I say is unimportant. The purpose is to bring me to the Father, to that peace inside. In the past it was me-centered. I would race through the rosary simply reciting a bunch of words. Today the rosary is a God-centered devotion. After I share this at missions, many people tell me they repeat the rosary when they go to bed, so they can fall asleep.

I use my sixth form of prayer when I am afraid. I pray that what I fear the most will happen — if it is God's will. Fear is our greatest enemy. We must deal with it or it will rule our lives. The more we feed fear, the bigger it gets. Recently, I was in San Diego, California, when my sister was diagnosed with melanoma, the cancer that was the ultimate cause of my dad's death. She urged everyone in the family to have a checkup. When the doctor looked at the mole I had on my leg, he said, "It doesn't look very good." What I heard him say was that I had six months to live. I became so fearful I even chose the priest who would preach at my funeral. I was filled with fear; it was a horrifying experience. I finally turned to prayer. My prayer is that when I'm really afraid, I pray that what I fear the most will happen if it is God's will, and if it happens, may I accept it. When I said this prayer, God took the fear from me. I had to wait three days for the test results. One of the longest days in our life is when we're are waiting for a doctor's call. If I hadn't given my fear to God, I'd have been a basket case before I was told the diagnosis was benign.

This is a marvelous prayer for those who suffer from the fear of abandonment. Individuals who fear abandonment tend to smother those they love and often drive them away. They create an environment that causes what they most fear to happen — a sort of self-fulfilling prophecy. By turning our fears over to God, we become focussed on God's love within. In this way we deal with our real problem — our fear.

There are two other prayers I occasionally use which involve scripture from the New Testament. I am not one who simply studies the scriptures. Instead I pray over them, and I urge others to study them and pray over them as well.

The first of these is a contemplation prayer. It requires us to use our imagination. Many of us use our imaginations quite often in other ways. We daydream throughout the day as we listen to music, drive through town, or sit in a lecture. I learned to be a fairly decent preacher from the years I taught young people in high school because I realized that if I didn't talk to their hearts, they daydreamed. If I talked to their heads, their minds were a million miles away.

I use my imagination at night. I often have a difficult time getting to sleep because my mind is so active. If I don't bring problems to God through prayer, I start thinking about them, and the problems become bigger the longer I lie there. What begins as a problem at ten o'clock at night becomes a disaster by two in the morning. In order to get to sleep I escape into a fantasy world. I have a mental videocassette library of fantasies in my head, and each night I select one for that evening's escape. On some nights I make believe I'm running for President. On a good night I'm asleep before the New Hampshire primary. On bad nights I'm running for re-election. Recently, I've been developing one where I live on a farm. It has a trout lake, a huge vegetable garden, and several animals. I have a white German shepherd dog that follows me wherever I go. Some days I'm working in the garden, and other days I'm getting eggs from the chickens or taking care of the rabbits.

These fantasies calm me down, and soon I fall asleep. However, I hope some day one of my fantasies will become a reality. I will retire in a rural parish and spend my time growing vegetables, tending animals, catching fish, and going for long walks with my dog.

This imagination is something each of us has, and we can use it when we contemplate the scriptures. The story of the rich, young man who would not give up his wealth to follow Jesus is a passage I use when I'm having difficulty letting go of something in my life.

Once a man came to Jesus. "Teacher," he asked. "What good thing must I do to be the best person I can be?"

"Why do you ask me concerning what is good?" answered Jesus. "There is only one who is good. Keep the commandments if you want to enter eternal life."

"What commandments?" he asked.

Jesus answered. "Do not murder. Do not commit adultery. Do not steal. Do not lie. Honor your father and mother. Love your neighbor as yourself."

"I have obeyed all these commands," the young man replied. "What else do I need to do?"

Jesus said, "If you want to be the best person you can be, go and sell what you have, and give the money to the poor, and you shall have riches in heaven. Then come and follow me."

When the young man heard this, he went away sad because he was very rich.

This is the good news of Jesus Christ.

If Jesus were to meet each one of us, like with the rich young man, he would find something in our lives that prevents us from trusting God. It is these "things" that prevent us from becoming more spiritual. All of us have at least one thing in our life we can't let go of. The question is, "Do we know what that one thing is?"

I know two fine and wonderful men who are pouring all their money into a business that will never make it. They're basically throwing money into a sinkhole and will eventually go bankrupt. The driving force behind their unfortunate actions is that each one of them has made the business the absolute in his life. They're driven to have this business because it gives their lives meaning.

We often make relative things absolutes. However, the only real absolute in our life is God's love. Everything else is relative. When we make relative things absolute and the absolute relative, we have real problems in our life.

For example, I don't need to be a Catholic or a Jesuit to find God. I could be Protestant, Jewish, or a Moslem. Nature could be my church. The only absolute is God. I don't have to be a Jesuit to find peace. I could be a Franciscan, but I don't think I could be a Diocesan.

Those are relative values. It saddens me when I hear people say, "I couldn't live my life without her," or "If something happened to him, my life would be over." They're making the other person an absolute in their lives. They're making the other person a god. By hanging onto people or things we've made absolute and refusing to let them go, we set ourselves up for so much pain.

Now let us use our imagination for a moment and participate in this contemplation. Picture yourself meeting Jesus. How does he look to you? What kind of eyes does he have? Are they blue, gray, brown? What color is his hair? What length is it? What style? How is his nose shaped? Now create an image of what you look like to yourself and place yourself in this conversation with Jesus. You ask him, "What do I have to do to really follow you?" What will Jesus ask you to surrender, to let go of?

Jesus could read people's hearts, and as he did in the parable of the rich young man, he can look at each one of us and know what it is that prevents us from surrendering and trusting God in our lives.

For the young man in the story, it was his wealth. That was his absolute, and he could not give it up. Material possessions aren't bad; they're gifts from God. However, they can only celebrate the spiritual. They can't substitute for it.

What have you made absolute in your life? What do you need to let go of?

I use this prayer often because I'm an obsessive, compulsive person and can make anything an absolute. As a result, I must surrender many things because they start owning me. Whenever we become extremely worried about our children, spouses, or careers, we can come to prayer and find that if we give God the time, God will relieve us of our burden. This prayer was my greatest tool in breaking my need to be a rescuer.

As I've said, all my life I've been a rescuer of the most troubled people around. There could be two of the most burdensome people in a city, and I'd find a way to locate them. The more they need me, the more I'm there. This prayer has been a great help in releasing me from my rescuing. I've learned at last to let go of these people. I asked God to care for them and turned them over to God. Too often I see that when others have problems, they call a friend who will agree with them. It's better if they take their problems through this prayer to God.

The final prayer is a meditation which is different from a contemplation. In a meditation there are three realities: our experience, the Word of God in scripture, and the living God working within our hearts.

Each of us needs to place ourselves in the presence of God and think of something we've done that we have the greatest difficulty forgiving ourselves for or a hatred we cannot release. Think of something that has caused you shame. In shame, we think we are a mistake. In guilt, we feel we've done something wrong. Is there anything about your past that, when you're reminded of it, gives you a feeling of worthlessness throughout your whole body — your whole being? That's a shame attack. What is the hardest deed in our past to forgive? What is the one thing that keeps bothering us, that comes back when we let our guard down? If we had the opportunity to live our lives over again, what one thing would we change? I have a few of them in my life, a few things I pray to God that nobody ever finds out.

Think about the one deed in your life that is the hardest to give over to God. Place yourself in God's presence, and as you think about it, read through the story of the prodigal son, a story Jesus told to illustrate how much God loves us.

The story of the prodigal son is the message of THE GOD WITHIN. This is Jesus telling us how much God loves us. How much love there is within. It exemplifies the kingdom within that we must all discover.

We need to listen to these words and bring them to that which we can't forgive within ourselves. The son doesn't go back because he likes his father or wants to be with him. He doesn't go back because he's sorry. The only reason he goes back is because he's hungry. The father doesn't wait for him but runs out to greet him. He doesn't give a lecture or sermon. He doesn't even give his son a penance. He kisses and hugs his son because he loves him. Then the celebration begins.

I mentioned earlier that the sacrament of reconciliation is a celebration of love. A great way to prepare for this sacrament is to contemplate on the story of the prodigal son.

There was a man who had two sons. The younger one said to his father, "Father, give me now my share of the property." So the father divided the property between his two sons. After a few days, the younger son sold his part of the property and left home with his money. He went to a far away country where he wasted his money on reckless living. He spent everything he had. Then a severe famine spread over that country, and he was left without a thing. So, he went to work for one of the citizens of that country who sent him out to his farm to take care of the pigs. He wished he could fill himself with the bean pods the pigs ate, but no one gave him any.

At last he came to his senses and said, "All my father's hired workers have more than they can eat. And here I am about to starve. I will get up and go to my father and say, 'Father, I have sinned against God and against you. I am no longer fit to be called your son. Treat me as one of your hired workers.'"

So he got up and started back to his father. He was still a long way from home when his father saw him. His heart was filled with pity, and he ran to his son. He threw his arms around his son and kissed him.

"Father," the son said. "I have sinned against God and against you. I am no longer fit to be called your son." But his father called his servants. "Hurry," he said. "Bring the best robe and put it on him. Put a ring on his finger and shoes on his feet. Then go and get the prize calf and kill it, and let us celebrate with a feast for this son of mine was dead, but now he is alive. He was lost, but now he has been found."

And so, the celebration began.

This is the way God loves us. If any of us has a difficult time believing that God forgives us, all we have to do is just look at this passage and pray over it until we hear it with our heart and then let God work within us. Our purpose on this earth is to love ourselves and each other for we are made in the image of God. That is our journey.

One of the consequences of taking to heart this message is that you will systematically fire every member of your "committee." When you routinely listen with your heart, absent an agenda, and respond to those around you with love, when the most important person in your life is yourself, when you are open to the love within you, you will experience a sense of freedom you have never known before.

It's been more than a decade since I spent that year walking the beach in Santa Barbara. The years have been demanding and exciting. My faith in a personal God has been rooted in my heart, and it has been my pleasure to bring comfort to the lives of many thousands. My message, that God is love and that we must all discover the kingdom within, has remained unchanged from the beginning, though over the years I have reexamined elements of it, widened the focus, and fine-tuned my interpretation.

A mother I know deals with her very young children's jealousy when she shows love to another sibling by telling them that there is always enough love.

She's right. The more we love, the more we can love, and the more love there is. The love within us, the kingdom, flows out from us to embrace everyone around us, to affect every aspect of our life. It begins and remains in our relationship with ourself.

It is all within us; the wonderful things that happen outside of us are a result of what has taken place within us.

GOD IS LOVE AND LOVE IS ETERNAL.

Notes

✝

Notes

✝

The God Within includes Father Tom Allender's thoughts on spirituality versus religion, the tools of spirituality, fear versus faith, how to achieve family spirituality, releasing anger, and the role of the sacraments and prayer in our lives.

<table>
<tr><td rowspan="10">O R D E R F O R M</td><td></td><td>Quantity</td><td>Amount</td></tr>
<tr><td>The God Within (Donation of $20.00 each)</td><td></td><td></td></tr>
<tr><td>$3.00 for Shipping & Handling (per book)
(Allow 4 weeks for delivery)</td><td>Total</td><td></td></tr>
</table>

☐ **Check** (Payable to **Agape Ministry, Inc.**) ☐ Visa ☐ MasterCard   Expr. Date ☐☐☐

☐☐☐☐☐☐☐☐☐☐☐☐☐☐☐☐ Card Num

Signature Required for Credit Card

Print Name   Telephone Numb

Address

City/State/Zip

Mail/FAX: MW Publishing, P.O. Box 3678, Phx., AZ, 85030, 602.241.140

Cut Here ☞

The God Within includes Father Tom Allender's thoughts on spirituality versus religion, the tools of spirituality, fear versus faith, how to achieve family spirituality, releasing anger, and the role of the sacraments and prayer in our lives.

<table>
<tr><td rowspan="10">O R D E R F O R M</td><td></td><td>Quantity</td><td>Amount</td></tr>
<tr><td>The God Within (Donation of $20.00 each)</td><td></td><td></td></tr>
<tr><td>$3.00 for Shipping & Handling (per book)
(Allow 4 weeks for delivery)</td><td>Total</td><td></td></tr>
</table>

☐ **Check** (Payable to **Agape Ministry, Inc.**) ☐ Visa ☐ MasterCard   Expr. Date ☐☐☐

☐☐☐☐☐☐☐☐☐☐☐☐☐☐☐☐ Card Nu

Signature Required for Credit Card

Print Name   Telephone Numl

Address

City/State/Zip

Mail/FAX: MW Publishing, P.O. Box 3678, Phx., AZ, 85030, 602.241.14